D0849205

Securitized Insurance Risk: Strategic Opportunities for Insurers and Investors

Edited by Michael Himick,
Meridian Communications,
and Sylvie Bouriaux, Chicago Board of Trade

Glenlake Publishing Company, Ltd.
Chicago • London • New Delhi

AMACOM
American Management Association
New York • Atlanta • Boston • Chicago • Kansas City
San Francisco • Washington, D.C.
Brussels • Mexico City • Tokyo • Toronto

This publication is designed to provide accurate and authoritative information in regard to the subject matter covered. It is sold with the understanding that the publisher is not engaged in rendering legal, accounting, or other professional service. If legal advice or other expert assistance is required, the services of a competent professional person should be sought.

AMACOM
American Management Association
New York · Atlanta · Boston · Chicago · Kansas City · San Francisco · Washington, D.C.
Brussels · Mexico City · Tokyo · Toronto

Contents

Part II: The (Old and New) Market Players

Contributors

Richard H. Bernero
Richard H. Bernero is vice president in the Insurance Products Group at
Bankers Trust, which Bankers Trust recently entered into a definitive
agreement to sell to RR Holding Company (a KKR entity controlling
Rhine Reinsurance). Bankers Trust will retain a minority interest in the
combined entity, and both Bankers Trust and Rhine Re foresee significant
business opportunities in continuing to work together after the sale. Mr.
Bernero joined Bankers Trust in 1992 and has held a variety of responsibilities in the Insurance Products Group since that time. He is currently
involved in structuring and new product development for the group, with
an emphasis on weather-related products (catastrophe bonds/swaps and
temperature derivatives), and has responsibility for client coverage for the
Americas and Bermuda. He has been involved in structuring, pricing, and
placement issues related to the securitization of insurance risk, including
liaising with credit rating agencies and catastrophe modeling firms. Mr.
Bernero was a member of the CBOT Advisory Board for the various PCS
catastrophe insurance options contracts and has responsibility for
Bankers Trust's membership in the Bermuda Commodities Exchange. He
is a director of BT Insurance Corporation and BT Life Insurance
Corporation and vice president and officer of BT Risk Intermediaries.
Prior to joining Bankers Trust in 1992, Mr. Bernero worked at JP Morgan
with the Global Distribution and Marketing team, offering quantitative
analytics and foreign exchange risk management products to corporations
and pension funds. Mr. Bernero graduated from Brown University in
1990 with a BA in material science engineering and a BA in international political economics.

Sylvie Bouriaux
Sylvie Bouriaux is manager of the Research and Product Development
Group for financial instruments at the Chicago Board of Trade. Her group

currently focuses on the development of new products in the equity area, in the insurance market, and in the real estate market. Prior to joining the Chicago Board of Trade in 1989, Ms. Bouriaux was assistant professor in economics at Rhode Island College in Providence. She earned a doctorate in economics from the University of Paris, France, and received an MA in economics from the University of Chicago. Ms. Bouriaux is a member of the Futures Industry Association and is a part-time faculty member at DePaul University in Chicago, where she teaches in the MBA program.

Michael P. Goldman

Michael P. Goldman is a partner in the Corporate Insurance Group of the Chicago law firm of Katten Muchin & Zavis, where his practice is concentrated on the corporate representation of insurance companies and other insurance entities, with a focus on acquisitions, divestitures, and corporate reorganizations (including demutualization); the regulation of insurance company investment practices, including the use of derivative instruments and strategies; and the structure and regulation of alternative risk financing mechanisms and complex reinsurance arrangements, including insurance securitization and derivatives. He also represents investment banks, commercial banks, private equity funds, derivatives dealers, investment advisors, and other sectors of the financial services industry, with respect to insurance company relationships and transactions. Mr. Goldman authored the National Association of Insurance Commissioners (NAIC) statutory accounting rules for insurance futures and options, and his article "A Regulatory Overview of the Insurance Industry's Use of OTC Derivatives" appeared in the May/June 1996 edition of *Derivatives (Tax Regulation Finance)*. In addition, he has been appointed to industry advisory and technical resource committees for various NAIC task forces and regularly provides counsel to the Illinois Department of Insurance regarding emerging insurance regulatory issues. Mr. Goldman is also a member and past chair of the Insurance Companies Committee and Regulatory Liaison Subcommittee of the Illinois CPA Society. Mr. Goldman graduated with high honors from the University of Illinois with a bachelor of science degree in accountancy and became a certified public accountant in 1982. He received his juris doctor degree, with honors, from Loyola University of Chicago School of Law and was admitted to the Illinois Bar in 1985.

Greg Hagood
Greg Hagood is executive director of Willis Corroon Catastrophe Management, a fund management subsidiary of Willis Corroon Group dedicated to institutional investments in securitized insurance risk. Mr. Hagood began his career at AT&T as an account executive and market analyst, performing revenue forecasting and developing competitive strategies. He joined Bear, Stearns & Co. in 1993, where he managed the mortgage servicing trading desk. His responsibilities included trading and brokering mortgage servicing portfolios, advising on mortgage banking mergers and acquisitions, and structuring hedging instruments for institutional clients. Mr. Hagood joined Willis Corroon North America in February 1997. He co-founded Bayhead Advisors LLC in 1995, where his responsibilities included investor relations and operations management. He received his BS in finance from the University of Tennessee.

Bernard L. Hengesbaugh
Bernard L. Hengesbaugh is executive vice president and chief operating officer for Chicago-based CNA, a major U.S. insurance products and insurance-related services organization. He is responsible for the overall performance of CNA's eight operating departments. Prior to assuming his current responsibilities, Mr. Hengesbaugh served as president and chief operating officer for CNA's Specialty Operations Department, vice president and controller for CNA's Field Operations Department, and vice president of the Corporate Accounting Division in the Financial Services Department. Prior to joining CNA, he was a partner with Deloitte & Touche. He is a certified public accountant and a member of the American Institute of CPAs. He is also a member of the board of directors of the Joint Commission on Accreditation of Healthcare Organizations. He earned a master's degree in business administration from Indiana University and a bachelor of science degree from St. Joseph's College.

Donna Hill
Donna Hill is currently involved with a start-up company, as yet unnamed, that will specialize in the area of alternative risk transfer. She is an associate editor of *Risk Financier* and has written widely on alternative risk transfer issues. Previously, she has served as a director at Swiss Re; prior to that, she worked at Goldman Sachs. Ms. Hill graduated from Yale University with a BS in molecular biophysics and biochemistry and holds an MA in international economics and finance from Brandeis University. She is fluent in several languages and has taught risk

management and bank accounting courses in Stavropol, Russia, to a group of bankers on a program funded by the U.S. Agency for International Development.

Michael Himick
Michael Himick is president of Meridian Communications, Inc., a specialist developer of knowledge-based books and marketing communications for the executives, entrepreneurs, and experts leading today's information economy. Mr. Himick has served as developmental editor for an illustrated history commemorating the Chicago Board of Trade's sesquicentennial anniversary, co-authored a book introduction on venture capital funds, and advised numerous companies on marketing communications strategy. Prior to founding Meridian, he was chief editor at the Chicago Board of Trade, where he published, among other derivatives work, over a dozen articles on the exchange's catastrophe insurance options. Mr. Himick currently serves as executive editor of the forthcoming *Risk–Fitzroy Dearborn International Encyclopedia of Derivatives: Futures, Options, Swaps, and Other Tools of Risk Management* (Risk Books and Fitzroy Dearborn Publishers) and as editorial director of the Know More™ series of business insight books (Five:30 Books).

Tom Hutton
Tom Hutton is president and chief executive officer of Risk Management Solutions, Inc. (RMS), a leading provider of risk modeling software and consulting advisory services to insurers and other financial institutions globally. He is an active speaker and author on issues ranging from risk management to risk securitization and has advised numerous RMS clients with respect to securitization and capital markets risk finance and risk transfer opportunities. Prior to RMS, he was a management consultant at McKinsey & Company, Inc. He received BA and MS degrees from Stanford University and an MBA from the Harvard Business School.

Frank Majors
Frank Majors is managing director of Willis Corroon Catastrophe Management, a fund management subsidiary of Willis Corroon Group dedicated to institutional investments in securitized insurance risk. Mr Majors began his career as a reinsurance broker for Wilcox, Inc., the reinsurance subsidiary of Johnson & Higgins. He joined Willis Faber North America as assistant vice president in the Marine, Aviation, International, and Surety Division in 1993 and was named divisional director of the

Retrocession Division of Willis Faber & Dumas in 1996. His primary responsibility was developing and brokering alternative risk transfer contracts, including derivative-based and financial reinsurance agreements. Mr. Majors co-founded Bayhead Advisors LLC in 1995 to invest in CBOT catastrophe options. His responsibilities there included formulating investment strategy and overseeing risk management. He holds a BA in economics from Vanderbilt University and an MBA in finance from Vanderbilt's Owen Graduate School of Management.

David K. A. Mordecai

David K. A. Mordecai is vice president of financial engineering at AIG Risk Finance. Formerly, he was a director and the product manager for rating catastrophic risk bonds, synthetic notes, and credit and insurance derivatives at Fitch IBCA. As the lead analyst for insurance-linked securities, he developed rating analytics and performed probability and statistical analysis related to event risk and catastrophic risk transactions as well as model validation/verification and due diligence of the risk modeling firms. Mr. Mordecai is currently completing a PhD at the University of Chicago Graduate School of Business, researching credit arbitrage, intermediation, and the pricing, allocation, and distribution of event risk in the reinsurance and capital markets. He received an MBA in finance from the New York University Stern Graduate School of Business and has over ten years of experience as a capital markets professional. Mr. Mordecai's chapter is based on his presentation at the 1998 Risk Conference in London and New York, "Innovations in the Mechanisms for Securitization of Catastrophic Insurance Risk."

Adam Parkin

Adam Parkin is a general manager with The Rangeley Company, a firm that assists in the development of specialist investment management companies. Previously, he had been a director of American Express Bank Asset Management Limited, Foreign and Colonial Management Limited, and John Grovett & Co. Limited. Most recently, he was managing director of LCF Edmond du Rothschild Fund Management Limited. Mr. Parkin's investment management experience incorporates pioneering use of derivatives, including, in 1991, the first authorized futures and options funds launched in the United Kingdom. He has served as a board member of the UK Futures and Options Association and as chairman of the UK Managed Futures Association.

Michael J. Pinsel

Michael J. Pinsel is a senior associate in the Corporate Insurance Group of the Chicago law firm of Katten Muchin & Zavis, where his practice is concentrated primarily in the corporate and regulatory representation of insurance companies and other insurance entities, focusing on such entities' internal corporate governance and shareholder relationships; the formation and capitalization of insurance companies; the structure and reorganization of insurance holding company systems; the regulation of insurance company investment activities, including the use of derivative instruments; acquisitions of and venture capital investments in insurance companies and related entities; and the structure and regulation of alternative risk financing mechanisms, including insurance securitizations and derivatives. Mr. Pinsel has spoken on the regulation of alternative risk financing mechanisms and insurance companies' derivatives activities and co-authored an article entitled "A Regulatory Overview of the Insurance Industry's Use of Over-the-Counter Derivatives" that appeared in the May/June 1996 edition of *Derivatives (Tax Regulation Finance)*. Mr. Pinsel graduated cum laude from Duke University in 1988 with bachelor of arts degrees in economics, psychology, and religion. He received his law degree from the University of Chicago Law School and was admitted to the Illinois Bar in 1991.

Natalie Spadaccini Rosenberg

Natalie Spadaccini Rosenberg is an associate in Corporate Insurance Group of the Chicago law firm of Katten Muchin & Zavis. Ms. Rosenberg's practice is concentrated on the representation of insurance industry organizations in connection with corporate, commercial, and regulatory matters, including acquisitions, corporate reorganizations, and general corporate transactions; the regulation of insurance company investment practices, including the use of derivative instruments and strategies; and the securitization of insurance risk. Ms. Rosenberg graduated cum laude from Carleton College in 1991 with a bachelor of arts degree in political science. She received her juris doctor degree cum laude from Northwestern University School of Law in 1997 and was admitted to the Illinois Bar and to the United States District Court for the Northern District of Illinois in that same year.

Richard L. Sandor, PhD

Richard L. Sandor, PhD, is chairman of Hedge Financial Products, Inc., a wholly owned subsidiary of CNA Financial Corporation specializing in the securitization of insurance risks. Prior to the creation of Hedge

Financial, Dr. Sandor held senior executive positions in the financial services industry. For more than three years, he was vice president and chief economist at the Chicago Board of Trade, during which time he earned a reputation as the "principal architect of interest rate futures markets" for his work on the Treasury bond futures and options contracts, Treasury note futures contract, and others. He was a faculty member of the School of Business Administration at the University of California, Berkeley, and held a faculty position at Stanford University. Dr. Sandor currently serves as second vice chairman of the Chicago Board of Trade, on the International Advisory Board of the Marché à Terme International de France and the Financial Products Advisory Committee of the Commodity Futures Trading Commission, as a member of the board of directors for the Center for Sustainable Development in the Americas, and as an expert advisor to the United Nations Conference on Trade and Development on tradeable entitlements for carbon dioxide. Between 1991 and 1994, he was a nonresident director of the Chicago Board of Trade, where he was chairman of the Clean Air Committee developing the first spot and futures markets in environmental contracts. He also served as vice chairman of the Insurance Committee and was one of the authors of the catastrophe and crop insurance futures and options contracts. Dr. Sandor received his bachelor of arts degree from the City University of New York, Brooklyn College, and earned his PhD in economics from the University of Minnesota.

The Convergence of the Insurance and Capital Markets

Richard L. Sandor, PhD
Hedge Financial Products

"The trading of property catastrophe risk using standard financial instruments such as options and bonds enables insurance companies to hedge their exposure by transferring risk to investors, who take positions on the occurrence and cost of catastrophe. Although these property catastrophe risk instruments are relatively new products, they have already established an important link between the insurance industry and the U.S. capital market."
—Sarah Borden and Asani Sarkar, Federal Reserve Bank of New York

Consolidation is occurring in all segments of the insurance industry. In short order, Zurich acquired Farmers, St. Paul bought USF&G, Exel purchased MidOcean Reinsurance Co., and Benfield Group merged with Greig Fester. The trend continued in the second quarter of 1998 with the acquisition of General Re by Berkshire Hathaway and the establishment of Lehman Re in Bermuda with an initial capitalization of $500 million. Such ventures suggest that insurers, reinsurers, and intermediaries are all in stronger positions to deal with a catastrophic event. Indeed, few insurance executives would openly contest the image of an industry that is much more capable of absorbing both current and future property/casualty risk.

Nonetheless, the traditional markets still do not have the capacity to provide for ever-increasing catastrophe losses. Thus, the media indicate that insurance executives are actively seeking alternative forms of risk transfer, and the industry is rapidly gaining both expertise and experience in the insurance derivatives markets. This book provides a complete working kit to the reader interested in learning more about insurance securitization. The first few chapters give an overview of current developments in securitization and commoditization in the insurance industry. Specific instruments and their use are discussed by those who have developed or underwritten them. A thorough discussion of the legal and regulatory environment for these instruments is also provided. Finally, various chapters provide important insights on these instruments' utilization, both by the insurance industry and by investors.

The Origin and Evolution of Markets: A Seven-Stage Process

The rationale for developing alternative risk transfer instruments that complement traditional reinsurance is better understood in a discussion of how markets arise and evolve. Like their commodity, equity, and bond predecessors, organized and OTC insurance markets did not burst spontaneously onto the scene. On the contrary, like any other good or service, they are responses to latent or overt demand. Their successful evolution requires the development of specific legal and institutional infrastructures. Once we readily understand the evolutionary process underlying all new markets, the convergence of the insurance and capital markets becomes more obvious.

Let's postulate a simple seven-stage process that describes how markets evolve. Concisely stated, the evolving stages include: (1) a structural economic change that creates the demand for capital; (2) the creation of uniform standards for a commodity or security; (3) the development of a legal instrument that provides evidence of ownership; (4) the development of informal spot markets (for immediate delivery) and forward markets (nonstandardized agreements for future delivery) in commodities and securities where "receipts" of ownership are traded; (5) the emergence of securities and commodities exchanges; (6) the creation of organized futures markets (standardized contracts for future delivery on organized exchanges) and options markets (rights but not guarantees for future delivery) in commodities and securities; and (7) the proliferation of OTC markets/deconstruction.

Importantly, this seven-stage process does not constitute an unalterable chain of events that markets must pass through sequentially. Rather, it is an analytical instrument that seems to fairly well describe the multiple forces that accrue over time and that sometimes develop into sophisticated and efficient markets. It does not purport to prove a causal connection, only to highlight a natural dialectic.

History is replete with market "evolutions" that can be analyzed using this seven-stage heuristic. Let's illustrate this process with a selected example from each of three market sectors: equity-capital, commodity, and fixed-income security. These examples, intended as nothing more than historical sketches, touch on the highlights of the market process under our review.

First, consider how the equity-capital market evolved. When Christopher Columbus "conquered" the New World, that "discovery" (from the European perspective) brought upon the world economy a fundamental structural change, in that the resulting Age of Discovery required financial capital. Initially, the instrument used to deploy capital was a "partnership," often devoted to specific purposes. The concept further evolved into the invention (and subsequent adoption) of the "limited liability corporation."

The Dutch East India Company was a novel creation that would become the archetype of the modern corporation. It unquestionably provided a more highly evolved "standard," as its "evidence of ownership" took the form of transferrable equity shares. With the innovation of shares came the need to efficiently convey these financial rights. In response, the next level of market evolution surfaced as an organized marketplace: the Amsterdam Stock Exchange (as well as its regional exchange precedents). Spot trading, in turn, spawned the first documented examples of futures and options trading.

Another example that seems to fit our simple seven-stage process is the evolution of agricultural commodities trading in America. In the nineteenth century, the United States simultaneously experienced population growth and westward expansion. This coupling embodied a fundamental structural change in national and regional economics. The bulging population on the East Coast translated into demand for new and additional food sources. The emerging agricultural sector in the Midwest would provide the supply, but capital was needed to finance the grain-in-storage that would be shipped east. Unorganized trading was followed by the formation of the Chicago Board of Trade (CBOT), which codified grain standards. Soon the warehouse receipt became accepted evidence of ownership, facilitating both raising capital and transferring ownership of the stored grain. Spot trading in wheat and corn evolved into forward trading. Organized futures trading began at the CBOT in 1865. Ultimately, options trading emerged, albeit much later.

A more modern yet another American variant of the seven-stage evolution process can be found in examining the market for mortgage-backed securities (or, what came to be called "collateralized mortgage obligations") in the 1970s. Via two of its agencies—the Federal Housing Authority (FHA) and the Veterans Administration (VA)—the U.S. government had guaranteed home mortgages and in doing so started a process that would help transform formerly nonmarketable loans (which tended to stay with the lending institutions) into a standardized financial instrument. Throughout most of the 1960s, financial institutions in the East (e.g., savings and loans) furnished much of the capital to the booming housing market in California and other parts of the United States. Although the standardized FHA/VA mortgages assured capital flows to that sector, the market was still inefficient. This was so for two primary reasons: (1) mortgages were sold individually or in small packages and (2) the buyer had to have individual documentation for each loan. Although the government guarantee prevented any ultimate default, there was no guarantee of timely payment of principal and interest during the foreclosure period. As inflation increased in the United States during the "credit crunch" times of 1966 and 1969, demand for capital was further exacerbated, which, in turn, promoted further standardization for mortgages.

With the formation of the Government National Mortgage Association (GNMA), the institutional infrastructure was in place to "bundle" small loans into a security collateralized by FHA/VA mortgages in which the U.S. government guaranteed timely payment of interest and principal. This collateralized mortgage obligation provided an efficient ownership receipt and conveyance vehicle. Soon thereafter, spot and forward market trading emerged, primarily among Wall Street dealers and mortgage bankers. Although informal, these markets performed functions similar to an organized exchange. The evolution continued when the world's first interest rate futures contract—based on the GNMA mortgage-backed security—was launched at the CBOT in 1975.

Insurance Markets

We are currently witnessing yet another variant of the seven-stage process with the emergence of organized and over-the-counter markets in insurance risks. A latent demand for this market emerged from a significant increase in both the frequency and severity of catastrophes that have occurred in recent times within the United States. Although it is difficult to conclusively infer that climate change may be responsible for generating some of these catastrophes, it is clear that structural changes such as population shifts to higher risk areas, coupled with an increase in coastal wealth, explain recent losses. Today, half of the U.S. population lives in disaster-prone areas. Table 1 on page 6 shows the impact of changing U.S. demographics on concentrations of risk and assets.

The rationale for developing alternative risk transfer tools in the insurance industry is easy to understand. The U.S. insurance industry has approximately $265 billion in available capital, which must cover property risks of $25-30 trillion as well as the casualty coverage associated with a $7 trillion economy. The arithmetic simply does not work. This is particularly true when projections suggest that a single catastrophic event in areas like Miami, Florida, or Orange County, California, could result in insured losses of $50-100 billion. On the other hand, the worldwide capital markets, with equities and fixed-income totaling more than $30 trillion, could easily absorb a hefty portion of risk from the insurance market. The arithmetic explains the potential need for new capital in the industry.

The development and extensive use of the "industry loss warranty" (ILW) in the London marketplace in the 1980s provided the basis for a uniformity. Industry loss warranties are fairly standardized traditional reinsurance policies, in that the indemnity received by the insurance company depends on the company's own loss trigger *and* upon an insurance industry catastrophic loss trigger. Other policy terms, such as the loss and development periods as well as the indemnity, are similarly standardized.

The spiral of issuance of these double-trigger policies is somewhat analogous to the development of a spot/forward market in catastrophe insurance. Subsequently, in 1992, the CBOT began trading futures contracts based on underlying "catastrophic" insurance industry loss ratios for specified states and regions within the United States. The product eventually evolved in 1995 into options contracts based on an index of aggregated loss estimates compiled by Property Claim Services (PCS), as it became obvious that the previous loss ratio measure did not adequately track insurance industry losses. In addition, the concept of an option became more popular and understandable to the insurance industry, as

Table 1 Changing U.S. Demographics Have Created New Concentrations of Assets and Risk

State	U.S. Census 1950 (in millions)	State	U.S. Census 1970 (in millions)	State	July Est. 1995 (in millions)
New York	14.8	California	20.0	California	31.6
California	10.6	New York	18.2	Texas	18.7
Pennsylvania	10.5	Pennsylvania	11.8	New York	18.1
Illinois	8.7	Texas	11.2	Florida	14.2
Ohio	7.9	Illinois	11.1	Pennsylvania	12.1
Texas	7.7	Ohio	10.7	Illinois	11.8
Michigan	6.4	Michigan	8.9	Ohio	11.2
New Jersey	4.8	New Jersey	7.2	Michigan	9.5
Massachusetts	4.7	Florida	6.8	New Jersey	7.9
North Carolina	4.1	Massachusetts	5.7	Georgia	7.2
Total	**80.2**	**Total**	**111.6**	**Total**	**142.3**

trading a combination of options can replicate a layer of reinsurance more effectively than can trading futures contracts.

A review of the growth of risk management tools in the interest rate and equity arenas strongly implies that we are poised for exponential growth in insurance securitization. The Chicago Board of Trade's invention of markets in interest rate futures and options in the 1970s, for example, helped spur the over-the-counter swaps and options market, which soared from less than $1 trillion in 1987 to almost $30 trillion in 1997. A similar pattern seems to emerge in catastrophe securitization, with over-the-counter catastrophe issues increasing from less than $200 million in June 1996 to over $2 billion by June 1998.

Over a 30-month stretch, 14 separate insurers—including U.S., European, Japanese, and Bermudian companies—securitized more than $2 billion in catastrophic insurance risk, using mechanisms such as catastrophe bonds, CatEPuts, capital surplus notes, exchange-traded catastrophe options, and over-the-counter swaps and options. At the same time, the exchange-traded catastrophe options market continued to grow, as the CBOT offered ever-growing alternative capacity to the insurance and reinsurance industry and as a new exchange was set up in Bermuda to trade instruments similar to the CBOT options. Figures 1 and 2 illustrate the growth of the alternative risk transfer tools both in the over-the-counter market and at the CBOT and compare their growth to the earlier development of OTC and exchange-traded interest rate instruments.

Lending even more reason for optimism about the future of insurance securitization, the financial and human capital committed by the firms participating in this market forms the basis of a self-fulfilling prophecy. The investment and commercial banks involved in securitized transactions include Merrill Lynch, Goldman Sachs, Chase Securities, and Donaldson, Lufkin & Jenrette. Lehman Brothers announced that it too will establish a significant presence in insurance derivatives. Domestic and European insurers and reinsurers such as AIG, CNA, Zurich, and Swiss Re have set up specialty units. Leading intermediaries such as Marsh McLennan, Aon, and Benfield Greig have also devoted substantial resources to these emerging markets.

The trend is clear. In spite of industry consolidation and a decreasing rate environment, securitization is growing and evolving. Hurricane and earthquake risk is readily being transferred to the capital markets. Hedge funds, pension funds, insurance companies, and high-net-worth individuals are buying these new types of assets and have extended their interest from single-year to multi-year risk.

Figure 1 PCS & OTC Catastrophe Issues

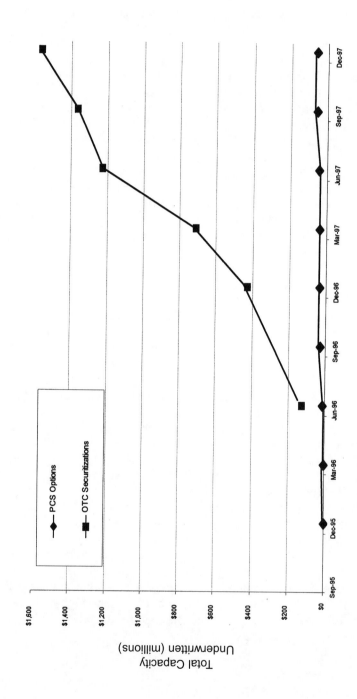

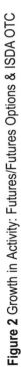

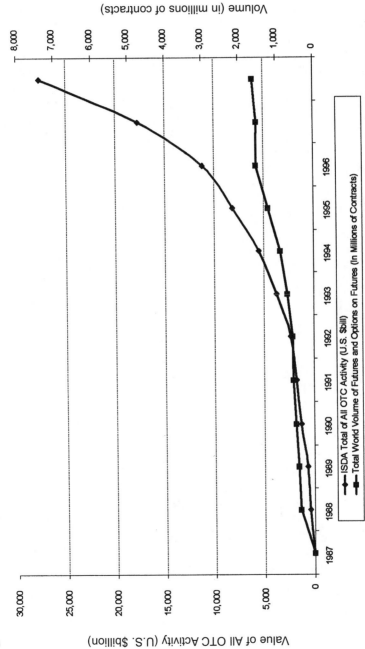

Figure 2 Growth in Activity: Futures/Futures Options & ISDA OTC

Note: Total of all activity numbers include interest rate swaps + currency swaps + interest rate options. Where data is missing for any of these categories, ISDA reported totals appear to reflect the sum of available data.

So far, most securitized transactions have targeted the catastrophe area. It is, however, only a matter of time before these parties begin to absorb additional types of property, life, and casualty risk. One can easily foresee securitization of environmental and health care risks. We already have witnessed insurance contracts linked to the number of barrels of oil spilled, the medical component of CPI, and the number of lives lost in an airplane crash. These indexes could easily be embedded in index-linked notes or similar instruments. From the percentage of occupancy of nursing homes to environmental emissions, the opportunities to securitize long-term casualty liabilities are enormous. We are truly at the dawn of an era that will witness remarkable opportunities for the organizations that participate in this process.

*****

Note: Portions of this chapter were drawn from other publications by the author, including "The Future of Securitization" (Ernst & Young's *Insurance Executive*, Summer 1998) and "The Role of the United States in International Environmental Policy" (in *Preparing America's Foreign Policy for the Twenty-First Century*, edited by David L. Boren and Edward J. Perkins, University of Oklahoma Press, forthcoming). See also "Insurance Derivatives: A New Asset Class for the Capital Markets and a New Hedging Tool for the Insurance Industry" (with Michael S. Canter and Joseph B. Cole, *Journal of Derivatives*, Winter 1996).

Part I
The New Risk
Transfer (and
Investment Portfolio)
Tools

Rethinking Risk: Across Traditional Boundaries

Donna Hill

As organizations design their risk management programs, they are increasingly likely to consider a total financial risk management approach, in lieu of an approach uniquely focused on insurance risk transfer. Rethinking risk across traditional boundaries requires that organizations identify those risks that could adversely affect their cash flow, net income, and capital strength. This identification process immediately takes the risk manager, treasurer, and chief financial officer beyond a discussion of risks that have traditionally been considered "insurable" to a broader scope of hazards, such as financial and political risks. A broader definition of risks to the organization in turn requires a much larger arsenal of tools to finance those threats (see figure 1-1). Hence, the continued evolution of the alternative risk transfer (ART) market.

Figure 1-1 Transferring Risk Across Traditional Boundaries: Is There an
Efficient Frontier?

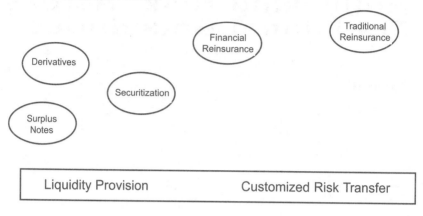

We Are All ARTists Now

The so-called ART market comprises alternative distribution channels
(i.e., direct marketing to corporate insureds) and alternative vehicles to
finance insurance risk (e.g., securitizations of insurance risk). The ART
market accounts for 40% of the commercial market and is growing at a
rate twice that of the traditional market (see figures 1-2 and 1-3).

Figure 1-2 Alternative Market Growth
Net Premium Written from 1988 to 1995

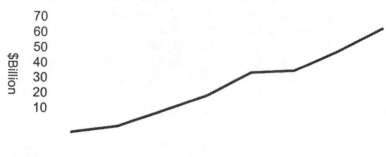

Source: Conning & Co.

Figure 1-3 Alternative vs. Traditional Market Growth:
Average Annual Percentage Growth in Net Premium Written

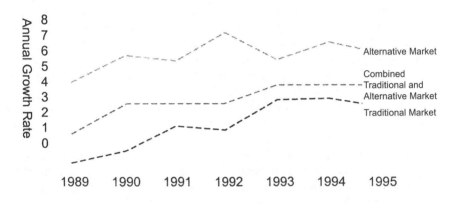

Sources: A. M. Best and Conning & Co.

Another way to consider the size of the ART market is to estimate the percentage of total risk financing costs embedded in reinsurance programs. According to a Swiss Re Sigma report, this represents approximately one-third of the total market in workers' compensation, two-thirds of the total market for medical malpractice, and approximately 40% of the total commercial auto and liability markets.

Table 1-1 Composition of the ART Market, 1995

Commercial	56.3%
Risk Retention Groups	0.8
Self-Insurance	16.6
Captives	7.6
Pools and Trusts	5.8
Private Retention	12.8

Source: Sigma

The rapid rate of growth in the ART market through the 1980s was driven primarily by concerns about both the availability and affordability of reinsurance coverage. These concerns have diminished in the current, relatively soft, market. In the 1990s, growth in the ART market has been driven by flexibility on the scope of coverage by primary insurers and reinsurers and by a more strategic approach to risk financing by corporations, often resulting in much higher retention levels. Lower volumes of premiums supporting higher layers of risk at softer prices do not bode well for the reinsurance industry. Consequently, leaders in the market are attempting to diversify their product lines from traditional reinsurance, in which a commodity product is subject to intense price competition, into higher value-added, structured risk financing products.

For example, consider the so-called insurance basket product, in which corporate insureds may commingle traditional insurance risks (property, liability, etc.) with financial risks (foreign exchange, interest rate, etc.) in a single vehicle. Bundling traditional lines with a financial component on an aggregate basis lowers the cost relative to insuring individual lines separately. Take the example of Honeywell, a multinational corporation that generates approximately $750 million in annual earnings, one-third of which is generated overseas.[1] Traditionally, Honeywell had placed its property, liability, and workers' compensation risks with different carriers and had hedged its foreign exchange exposures with the banks (see figure 1-4).

Figure 1-4 Traditional Program

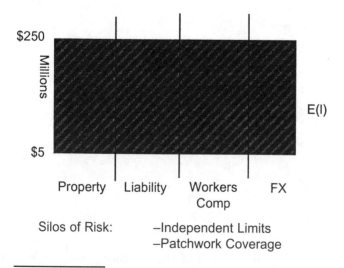

Silos of Risk: −Independent Limits
                 −Patchwork Coverage

---

[1] The Honeywell example was discussed in detail in *Forbes*, April 21, 1997.

An insurance basket offers a more efficient solution. Honeywell purchases a single, three-year insurance policy covering property, liability, workers' compensation, and currency exposures. There is a single retention—with an annual premium affording a 25% cost savings relative to the traditional program—covering a defined layer of losses (see figure 1-5). The multiyear program also affords lower frictional cost as losses are normalized over time. In addition to offering improved returns on risk-adjusted capital, due to the correlation effect across the different lines of risk, the basket product offers a potential "winner take all" market dynamic to the provider. That is, players with the financial expertise to price insurance baskets have the potential to grow their premium volume at the expense of those who do not.

Figure 1-5 Insurance Basket

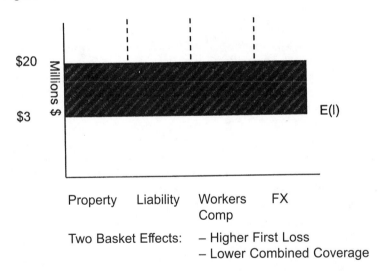

Two Basket Effects: – Higher First Loss
                       – Lower Combined Coverage

Corporate Demand for Risk Management Programs Crosses Traditional Boundaries

The Honeywell example portends a dramatic shift in the provision of risk management products in the insurance and reinsurance industries. Traditionally, insurers focused on insurable or event risk as their exclusive domain. Other types of financial risks, such as foreign exchange exposures, interest rate risk, or other types of balance sheet risk, were left to other financial intermediaries.

An integrated approach to risk management requires that an insured assess its aggregate risk appetite, set retentions accordingly for all categories of risk, and assess the utility of all risk-mitigating instruments ("financial" products as well as traditional insurance coverages). This approach facilitates the assessment of shareholder value-at-risk by taking a more comprehensive view of insurable risk. Corporate insureds expend less effort in evaluating risk coverage for a specific event and more effort developing comprehensive balance sheet protection. A number of insureds are known to be leaders in implementing so-called integrated risk management programs (see table 1-2). This list will surely grow.

Table 1-2 Some Integrated Risk Management Leaders

BC Rail	TRW	SmithKline Beecham	Coca-Cola
Rothman's	Guinness	BTR	Alcatel-Alsthom
Beckitt Coleman	Pechiney	Becton Dickinson	Siemens
Dalgetly	Sun Microsystems	Goldman Sachs	BBC
Norwest Bank	Jacob's Engineering	Medtronics	Huntsman Chemical
Honeywell	Pfizer	Sara Lee	Quaker Oats
Union Carbide	Lucent		

The institutions that are the pioneers in this integrated approach are most often found in the banking industry. Banking regulators examine global risks, rather than discrete risks, prompting banks to do the same. Banks are already proficient as managers of financial risk. Their exposure to credit, interest rate, foreign exchange, operating, and other types of risk requires a more comprehensive approach to risk management. Banks are thus increasingly positioned to compete with primary insurers and reinsurers to provide risk management services to their corporate clients.

Successful positioning by insurers requires that they adopt an approach to risk management unencumbered by arbitrary distinctions between insurable risks and other types of financial risks that are equally ruinous to the corporate balance sheet. A loss on the value of the investment portfolio due to interest rate movements may be no less severe to the corporate bottom line than a loss caused by a hurricane damaging an office building. Similarly, as insurers examine a broader array of risks, they must develop a broader array of risk-mitigating techniques. They must develop risk financing tools unencumbered by distinctions between policy coverages and nonpolicy coverages.

Structuring Risk Financing Tools Across Traditional Boundaries[2]

Traditionally, the banking industry has focused on financial risk management, both by constructing efficient investment portfolios and by employing increasingly sophisticated financial hedging strategies. The insurance industry has traditionally focused on event risks. Developments in the derivatives markets have blurred this distinction. Moreover, capacity constraints in the insurance markets (such that over the past decade insurance contracts often financed, rather than transferred, risk) have motivated the development of alternative risk transfer techniques.

Consider the example of risk of loss due to fire. This risk is typically evaluated as an insurable risk: purchase of a homeowners' policy provides protection against the risk of property loss. But this cover can be interpreted as another class of financial risk in the context of the convergence between insurance and the financial markets. The homeowners' insurance is, in effect, a put option. The policyholder pays a premium for an option to put his home to a counterparty (the insurance company will assume the liability of the fire-damaged house) when its market value has declined. Employing an integrated approach to risk management, using both insurance and financial tools, thus creates a larger supply of risk financing instruments to mitigate risk—in this case, a traditional insurance policy or a put option.

Similarly, an interest rate cap, typically considered a banking product, is, in effect, an insurance policy in an environment of rising interest rates. Recently, a California bank purchased a policy from a single insurer to protect itself against deterioration of a pool of mortgages, in lieu of a credit swap or derivative product from a bank. If insurers write cover against credit risk, why can't they provide protection against other types of financial risk?

Does this imply that derivative (specifically option) models may be used to price insurance and reinsurance? The current practice is to price premiums such that they reflect actual loss experience, providing for diversification across risks and periods of time. This approach incurs significant transaction costs. Under another paradigm, an insurance or reinsurance contract may be considered as an option on the liability portfolio of the insured or cedant. Just substitute "attachment point" for "strike

---

[2] See "Insurance and the Financial Markets" in *Convergence of the Financial and Insurance Markets*, edited by Mike Hanley, Emap Finance, London, 1996.

price." The premium paid for reinsurance cover is really an option by another name.

There are, however, difficulties in applying option theory to insurance. First, insurance loss distributions are not lognormal, undermining conventional pricing models. More important, the underlying asset—the profit stream generated by the insurance risk—is not actively traded. Furthermore, option theory is based on instantaneous measures of *discrete* changes, not aggregate measures based on the law of large numbers. Despite these distinctions, use of derivatives and insurance contracts as risk-mitigating instruments illustrates thinking across traditional boundaries of managing risk.

Capital Markets as a Source of Capacity

Another factor motivating insureds and insurers to rethink risk across traditional boundaries is capacity constraints within the insurance industry. Existing capital within the insurance industry is inadequate to finance insurance risks. Innovations in insurance risk finance, such as insurance ratings formulas, risk pools, captive arrangements, and finite risk contracts, have not closed the gap between supply and demand for insurance cover. Many view the capital markets as the biggest potential source of capacity (see figure 1-6). Consequently, a number of initiatives are underway to develop vehicles to access the capital markets for capital to underwrite insurance risks.

Figure 1-6 Capital Availability in the Markets

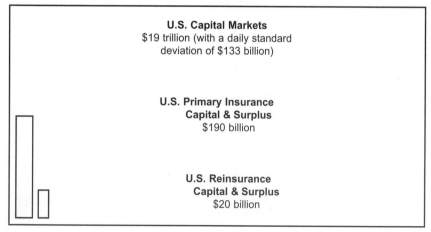

U.S. Capital Markets
$19 trillion (with a daily standard
deviation of $133 billion)

**U.S. Primary Insurance
Capital & Surplus**
$190 billion

**U.S. Reinsurance
Capital & Surplus**
$20 billion

In the United States, Nationwide Insurance Group closed a financing transaction intended to supplement the company's existing reinsurance. Nationwide agreed to sell up to $400 million in surplus notes to Morgan Guaranty Trust Company over ten years if the funds would be needed to cover catastrophic losses or to fund business expansion. A newly formed trust, Nationwide CSN Trust, was capitalized with an offering of trust notes and certificates to institutional investors. Proceeds of the offering were invested in $400 million of U.S. Treasury securities.

If Nationwide elects to sell its surplus notes, the notes will be exchanged with the trust for an equivalent amount of Treasury securities, which would then be contributed to Nationwide. This financing arrangement allows Nationwide to cover its catastrophic losses without tapping its surplus or limiting its underwriting. While surplus notes are not new, the structure of this financing is unique. This structure may have limited appeal for other insurers, however, such as stock companies that have other capital-raising alternatives. Furthermore, the transaction does not offer income statement protection comparable to a conventional reinsurance transaction.

Other possible risk financing techniques for a ceding insurer include issuing participating preferred stock with the dividend determined by the underwriting results of a particular line of business. In a variation of this theme, the insurer could issue debt with a nominal interest rate guaranteed and additional yield determined by underwriting results. Another alternative includes convertible debt, in which the ceding company issues debt convertible to common equity or surplus notes on the occurrence of a major insurance loss. Thus, the insurer locks in funding at a lower rate, as financing costs may rise following a major catastrophe. As the debt converts, the insurer's leverage declines and additional debt capacity is made available. The investors are compensated for the risk that catastrophic losses might drive down the insurer's stock price by an above-market interest rate or a more favorable exchange ratio.

The Business of Managing Risk

Distinctions between risk-mitigating products (such as insurance policies versus options) have become increasingly cosmetic as insureds seek comprehensive, cost-effective protection. The result is that insurers and other financial institutions are no longer unique intermediaries with exclusive market mandates. They are, together, in the business of managing risk.

Capacity constraints in the insurance and reinsurance markets, corporate demand for more efficient risk financing programs, and innovative uses of capital markets instruments are three factors motivating insureds and insurers to rethink risk across traditional boundaries. The next step in this evolution is the development of vehicles that can package insurance risk into discrete securities with finite risk, such that insurance risk may be traded and hedged in much the same way that interest rate risk is traded today.

Exchange-Traded Insurance Derivatives: Catastrophe Options and Swaps

Sylvie Bouriaux
Chicago Board of Trade

Michael Himick
Meridian Communications

When the Chicago Board of Trade (CBOT) opened the first-ever exchange-traded insurance derivatives market in December 1992, few people in the insurance industry fully understood how insurance "derivatives" might help manage insurance risk, just as few investors understood how holding insurance risk might benefit an investment portfolio. For many, insurance derivatives were just more financial voodoo, cooked up, according to one insurance industry editorial at the time, "to provide investors with another opportunity to gamble their money, and to further enrich the brokers who trade them."

Since then, the development of securitized and commoditized insurance risk structures and other capital markets risk management innovations has proceeded steadily. More and more insurers, reinsurers, brokers, bankers, and investors have committed their intellectual and financial resources to the convergence of the insurance and capital markets, as these developments are often called. Risk transfer products have evolved and improved, and people on all sides have ventured up the learning curve. Now, many in the insurance industry embrace the new tools as a potential strategic advantage. Institutional investors, both within and out-side the insurance industry, snap up catastrophe bond offerings. Even the hard-core insurance industry critics have relented, admitting that "all new sources of reliable capital should be welcomed with open arms and an open mind."

Still, despite the incredible development of securitized insurance risk instruments in general, the jury is still out on the efficacy of exchange-traded insurance derivatives in particular. While catastrophe bond place-ments have skyrocketed, exchange trading in catastrophe options, both at the CBOT and the more recently formed Bermuda Commodities Exchange (BCOE), has remained relatively light. Swap activity at the Catastrophe Risk Exchange (CATEX) has been similarly modest. Currently, insurers and investors seem to prefer structures that "securi-tize" the risk of specific insurance companies to structures—such as the risk indexes underlying standardized catastrophe options—that "com-moditize" insurance risk into a generically tradeable asset exchanged in a continuous and transparent market.

Clearly, though, exchange-traded insurance derivatives offer benefits that catastrophe bonds and other over-the-counter (OTC) instruments cannot match, such as immediacy, price transparency, and clearinghouse guarantees. Exchanges thus continue to introduce and improve their insurance risk management tools. The latest exchange-traded struc-tures—including the CBOT's proposed single-event catastrophe options—come closer than ever to blending exchange-traded standard-ization with OTC customization.

CBOT Catastrophe Options

The idea of using exchange-traded futures and options to mitigate insur-ance risks goes back at least as far as 1973.[1] Not until December 1992, however, did the CBOT create a functioning catastrophe insurance futures and options market. Initially, the rationale was to provide added capacity to an industry reeling from a succession of huge catastrophe losses, to build a new bridge between the insurance and capital markets upon which insurers and reinsurers could transfer catastrophic property risk to an enormous pool of private investor capital. Investors, for their

---

[1] See Robert Goshay and Richard Sandor, "An Inquiry into the Feasibility of a Reinsurance Futures Market," *Journal of Business Finance,* 1973, pp. 56-66.

part, would gain access to insurance risks—risks uncorrelated to the traditional investment asset classes. Alan Greenspan's U.S. congressional testimony can roil stocks and bonds, but there's little the Fed chairman can do to cause, or prevent, a hurricane.

The idea, too, was to bring the flexibility of derivatives to the insurance industry. Financial derivatives exist to allow users to adjust and manage risk. They give risk managers—including portfolio managers, balance sheet hedgers, and catastrophe underwriters—tools to divide or parcel various risks and move those risks in or out of a portfolio for an optimal risk configuration. In the insurance world, using catastrophe options to adjust the risks in a traditional reinsurance or retrocessional program might mean the ability to buy certain layers and durations of coverage for risks left exposed, hedge aggregate losses within retention levels, subtly adjust a risk profile, even geographically rebalance a book of business.

Key problems dogged the CBOT's first efforts, though. The CBOT's early attempt to commoditize insurance risk relied on a loss ratio index compiled from Insurance Services Office (ISO) data. That ISO index significantly underreported the Northridge earthquake, capturing only about a third of the insured losses estimated by Property Claim Services (PCS). The six-month loss development period after contract expiration didn't seem to allow sufficient time for reporting lags, either. Further, ISO issued reports to update the index only twice during each contract period, hardly allowing for the kind of continuous pricing that is a hallmark of exchange markets.

The CBOT also discovered that interest in its futures contracts was minimal. Options, more specifically option call spreads, better simulated the reinsurance layers that insurers, reinsurers, and reinsurance brokers were accustomed to. Call spreads involve buying and selling call options of the same expiration month but different strike prices. Call spread buyers, the equivalent of insurance buyers, buy calls at one strike price and simultaneously sell calls a higher strike price. Call spread sellers, the equivalent of insurance writers, sell calls at one strike price and simultaneously buy calls at a higher strike price. The strike prices represent the attachment points of the buyer's "coverage" (see figure 2-1). Almost all trading at the CBOT occurs as call spreads.

Index and Contract Evolution

The CBOT soon recognized its contracts' shortcomings and the market's preferred trading patterns. After sporadic development following insurance derivatives' introduction in December 1992, the CBOT introduced

Figure 2-1 Catastrophe Option Call Spreads as "Synthetic Reinsurance"

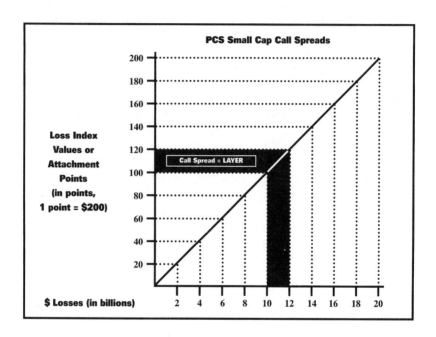

Source: CBOT

a second generation of insurance derivatives in September 1995 incorporating a much-needed redesign. Unlike the previous contracts, the current catastrophe options use PCS industry loss estimates—the industry standard for catastrophe loss estimates in the United States. The contract design was simplified and the development period was extended to twelve months, allowing greater time to more reliably estimate the final insured loss caused by a U.S. catastrophe. Futures were dropped entirely; only catastrophe insurance options were offered for trading (see tables 2-2 and 2-3 below for details on contract design and the PCS index).

Commentators in the insurance industry widely acknowledged these changes as substantial improvements. In the year immediately after the 1995 redesign, open interest rose spectacularly (see figure 2-2).[2]

---

[2] Open interest measures the number of options bought or sold that are still "open" in the market—positions not yet closed out by offset or settlement.

Moreover, improved contracts and increased trading gave market participants a chance to explore two unique benefits of exchange-traded insurance derivatives: immediacy and price transparency.

Figure 2-2 Catastrophe Option Open Interest, 9/95-12/96

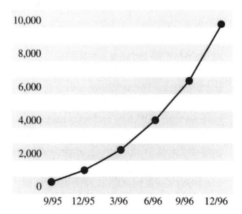

Source: CBOT

- *Immediacy.* Continuously traded catastrophe options theoretically allow insurers to adjust the risk in a book of business as catastrophic events threaten. For instance, on September 5, 1996, with Hurricane Fran threatening the East Coast of the United States, 3,308 catastrophe options traded at the CBOT. Catastrophe option sellers that day provided buyers with approximately $6.6 million in supplementary, last-minute coverage. That's not much by reinsurance standards, but it testifies to the willingness of option sellers to provide a market for immediate coverage even in the face of a hurricane—for an appropriately higher premium, of course. Should greater trading volumes develop, insurers and reinsurers could take better advantage of this eleventh-hour resource.

- *Price Transparency.* Proponents of exchange-traded derivatives like catastrophe options also hail the potential information edge gained from having a continuous open arena for the valuation of risk. In some markets, such as those for grains and U.S. government debt, the price transparency provided by exchange-traded futures and options markets actually forms the benchmark for all cash and OTC derivatives transactions conducted.

For example, look at how prices in the catastrophe options market responded to Hurricane Fran's threat. Trading on September 5, 1996, focused on the third-quarter Eastern contract at the 40/60 PCS index level, most likely because of the market's knowledge of Hurricane Hugo in 1989. A 40/60 call spread at the CBOT corresponds to $2 billion in aggregate industry losses in excess of $4 billion. Each point in each call spread represents $200 cash value. If aggregate industry losses fall between $4 billion and $6 billion, the buyer of a 40/60 spread is compensated for the difference between the trigger point and the index at settlement. If the index settles at 50, for example, representing $5 billion in aggregate industry losses, the buyer receives $2,000 per spread for the 10-point penetration into the 40/60 layer. If aggregate losses exceed the $6 billion exhaustion point, the buyer receives a total recovery of $4,000 per spread.

A week before Hurricane Fran, the bid price of the 40/60 spread—the price at which buyers wanted to get protection—was 1.0 point, a 5% quarterly rate on line (ROL).[3] The ask price—the price at which sellers wanted to provide protection—was 3.0 points, a 15% ROL. As it became obvious that Fran would make landfall, buyers began increasing their bids. Actual trades on the day Fran hit occurred at prices ranging from 3.4, a 17% ROL, to 4.0, a 20% ROL (see table 2-1). Ask prices remained somewhat firm prior to the event, holding above 3.0. Sellers, mindful of Hugo, apparently felt that 3.0 points represented the lowest acceptable compensation for assuming the risk posed by the storm.

In the days after Fran, buyers reduced their bids, sensing that Fran had not caused nearly the same damage as Hugo. Sellers responded, trading on September 11 for a premium of 1.0. These sellers probably thought that aggregate losses would not reach the $4 billion trigger and saw the trade as an opportunity to earn additional premium. In fact, the PCS index for the third-quarter Eastern loss period finished at 17.5, or $1.75 billion in aggregate industry losses, well below the $4 billion trigger.

---

[3] Rate on line is defined as the amount of premium paid for a cover, divided by the cover amount, expressed in percentage terms.

Table 2-1 Catastrophe Option Trades, Hurricane Fran 9/5/96

Contract	Call Spread/ Layer	# of Spreads	Premium	ROL
Sep Eastern	40/60	10	3.4	17%
Sep Eastern	40/60	10	3.5	17.5%
Sep Eastern	40/60	150	4.0	20%
Sep Southeastern	40/60	8	2.8	14%
Sep/Dec Eastern	40/60	700	4.0	Sep 19.5%; Dec .5%
Sep/Dec Eastern	40/60	96	4.5	Sep 22.5%; Dec .5%
Sep/Dec Eastern	40/60	670	5.0	Sep 24.5%; Dec .5%
Sep Eastern	80/100	10	2.0	10%
Total:		**1,654**		

Source: CBOT

Expansion of the CBOT's Insurance Complex

The CBOT plans to pursue its penetration into the insurance and reinsurance markets, first by expanding its current catastrophe insurance product line to include options based on single catastrophic events in the United States and abroad, then by listing instruments that track insurance companies' claims in other lines of business, such as marine, aviation, and satellite. While some of these products are still in the conceptual stage, single-event catastrophe insurance options are scheduled to be listed on the exchange in early 1999. In addition, the CBOT envisions listing Japanese earthquake options—triggered by the earthquake's physical characteristics—later that year.

The decision to offer options triggered by individual events in addition to the current index-based options stems from the observation that, although open interest in the current PCS catastrophe option complex has grown steadily (+65% in 1997), trading volume has expanded slowly (+6% in 1997) (see figure 2-3). Many factors, such as the steep learning curve created by the securitization of insurance risk and the restrictive regulatory environment for exchange-traded insurance instruments, can explain the slow but stable growth of these markets. The CBOT market also seems to have suffered from a lack of potential buyers, that is, large insurance companies, reinsurance companies, and "transformer" firms. These insurance companies have identified some inherent limitations in the currently traded PCS catastrophe options, such as the difficulty in estimating basis risk and in pricing the option.

Figure 2-3 Catastrophe Option Volume and Open Interest, 6/97-6/98

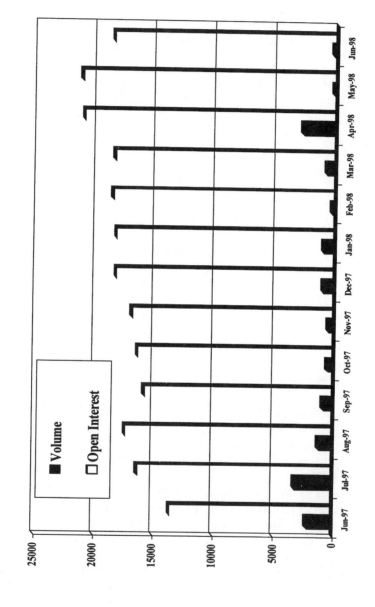

Basis risk in the currently traded PCS catastrophe options arises from two main sources: the individual company's loss exposure as compared to the industry's and the aggregation of catastrophic losses of different natures as captured by the PCS index. With the increasingly popular use of catastrophe modeling, insurance companies are becoming more and more adept at assessing their exposure and comparing it to that of the industry. The aggregation of catastrophic losses of different natures, however, may add an unwanted complication to loss estimation and to pricing the option.

In addition, a securitized "cash" market in the form of structured catastrophe-linked instruments has emerged and demonstrated tremendous energy. The payout of these instruments is generally tied to an individual loss trigger. In some instances, catastrophe bonds have been offered based on a PCS index trigger, but these have been difficult to place, sometimes resulting in the cancellation of the issue. Insurance companies who have indirectly issued cat bonds through transformer companies have been wary of the basis risk involved in using a PCS index trigger and generally prefer issuing bonds with a payout based on their own loss experience or on an industry single-event trigger. Some investors have also shied away from PCS index-based cat bonds because of the difficulty in pricing them.

The CBOT developed single-event catastrophe options to better respond to current market needs. On some occasions, options based on a single-event trigger will help hedgers (large insurers and reinsurers) minimize the basis risk they now face in using the currently traded PCS index-based options. In addition, single-event options will help bring in new market participants, as the fast development of catastrophe-based securities should provide some spillover business to the CBOT.

The CBOT's new PCS single-event options are similar in design to the current PCS index-based catastrophe options. The catastrophe must occur during a specific loss period (semi-annual or annual). The option expires at the end of a twelve-month development period following the loss period. The option's underlying instrument and the option premium are quoted similarly, too. Events are classified under two types of perils: earthquake and "atmospheric" (including hurricanes, tropical storms, wind, hail, and snow, as identified by PCS). The exchange plans to list single-event options for all nine regions and states already covered by the current PCS index-based catastrophe insurance options.

Design differences are as follows. First, the single-event options have a binary (fixed) payout feature of $10,000 when the option becomes in-the-money. Second, the single-event options will be listed sequentially.

Each option tracks a particular single event in the sequence at a particular strike. For instance, an option buyer could purchase a first-event 40 December call for Florida. In this case, the buyer's option would be in-the-money if at least one atmospheric event exceeded 40 index points ($4 billion, as estimated by PCS). In another instance, an option buyer could purchase a second-event 30 December call for Florida. In this case, the buyer's option would be in-the-money if at least two atmospheric events exceeded 30 index points ($3 billion, as estimated by PCS). Because the options are triggered by dual factors—event sequence and strike—one party's "first" event may differ from another party's "first" event.

Other Exchange-Based Risk Transfer Mechanisms

In the past two years, other exchange-based initiatives have followed in the CBOT's footsteps. First, in 1996, the New York Insurance Department approved the Catastrophe Risk Exchange (CATEX) as a reinsurance intermediary. Then, on November 12, 1997, the Bermuda Commodities Exchange (BCOE) opened its doors to trade insurance options conceptually similar to those already traded at the CBOT. Very few trades have been recorded so far on either exchange, as both markets are still very much in their infancy.

The Bermuda Commodities Exchange

The BCOE and the BCOE Clearing Corporation were created as the result of an original venture by the American Insurance Group (AIG), Guy Carpenter & Company, Chase Manhattan International Finance (an affiliate of Chase Manhattan Bank), and other smaller entities. To date, membership on the exchange has increased to about 30 firms. The BCOE is structured as a for-profit organization with its members as shareholders in the venture.

The instruments offered on the BCOE are conceptually similar to the CBOT's catastrophe options. Listings include cash options based on an underlying index and options based on a single loss event. These are expected to trade similarly. Where the CBOT and BCOE products differ is with respect to the underlying loss data contained in the index, the option design, and the margining of these options.

The BCOE options are based on a family of indexes created by Guy Carpenter & Company (GCCI). These indexes are computed as a loss-to-property-values ratio, based on insured homeowner losses due to atmospheric perils in particular regions of the United States over specific periods. The indexes are updated quarterly by IndexCo, LLC, a subsidiary of Guy Carpenter.

Tables 2-2 and 2-3 provide a comparison of the BCOE and CBOT options and their underlying indexes. The following points must be highlighted:

- The BCOE selected the GCCI as the underlying index for its options because the loss and claim data contained in these indexes can be geographically disaggregated at the zip code level, thereby refining the level of exposure information available to insurance companies. Note that the zip code feature is important from an informational standpoint, as it allows insurance companies that want to participate in the BCOE market to better compare their exposure to that of the industry as a whole. It is unlikely, however, that the BCOE will be able to support (from a liquidity standpoint) exchange-traded options that are based on indexes that track exposures at the zip code level. In fact, to date, the BCOE has only listed options based on regional and state indexes, similar to the CBOT. The disaggregation feature is more likely to be beneficial in the OTC market, which can better customize catastrophe option or bond programs.

- Guy Carpenter does not directly collect loss and exposure information from insurance companies, but receives the data from the Insurance Services Office. Although ISO has access to a substantial set of information from the insurance industry, some key insurance players, such as State Farm and Allstate, do not report claim, loss, or exposure data to ISO and are not expected to do so in the near future. Consequently, the GCCI indexes contain only about 25% of the insurance industry business in their sample, which is generally biased to the eastern region of the United States. In contrast, PCS routinely surveys 75-100% of the insurance industry when it estimates catastrophe losses.

- Finally, the GCCI family of indexes is published quarterly, but with a reporting lag of about four months. Lags in insurance companies' premium and loss reporting are inherent to the insurance business, as insurance companies generally compile information on a monthly or quarterly basis and then report it to diverse entities. What is generally accepted in the insurance business, however, does not necessarily bear well with the financial community, which is used to acting on fast and timely information. In contrast, because the PCS index is based on initial and subsequent survey estimates of insurance companies' losses, it is available daily and reported on a timely basis.

Table 2-2 CBOT vs. BCOE Options

Option Design	CBOT	BCOE
•Underlying Index	Property Claim Services (PCS) loss index	Guy Carpenter (GCCI) industry loss-to-value ratio
•Unit of Trading	1 index point = $200 (equivalent to $100 million in industry losses)	0.01% industry loss-to-value ratio[4]
•Geographic Coverage	9 geographic areas (Northeast, Southeast, East, Florida, Texas, Midwest, West, California, National)	7 geographic areas (Northeast, Southeast, Gulf, Mid/West, Florida, Texas, National)
•Types of Coverage	Aggregate losses Single-event losses	Aggregate losses Single and second loss
•Loss Periods	Quarterly/semi-annual/annual[5]	Semi-annual
•Settlement	Last business day of the 12th month following the end of the loss period	Variable. Up to 13 months from the end of the loss period. Early automatic exercise possible.
•Option Payoff Structure	For index-based options: depends on the ending value of the index	Binary ($5,000 when the option is in-the-money)
	For single-event options: binary ($10,000 when the option is in-the-money)	
Margin Requirements	CBOT imposes minimum initial margin calculated through the SPAN system, up to 20% of maximum exposure. Clearing firms may require additional margin.	100% posted up-front and held through expiration of the option ($5,000 per option)
	Variation margin posted on a mark-to-market basis	

Sources: CBOT, BCOE

---

[4] For instance, if the industry suffers a loss-to-value ratio of 2%, the index is valued at 200.
[5] For index-based options: California and Western are annual, all other regions are quarterly (National contract available in both). For single-event options: California and Western are annual, all other regions are semi-annual (National contract available in both).

Table 2-3 PCS vs. GCCI Indexes

	GCCI	**PCS**
•Index Provider	IndexCo, a wholly owned subsidiary of Guy Carpenter	Property Claim Services, a subsidiary of the Insurance Services Office
•Data Source	Claim, loss, and exposure data as reported to ISO by 39 insurance companies	Insurer phone survey Ground survey Internal estimates
•Percent of Insurance Business in Sample	About 25%	75% to 100%
•Lines of Business	Homeowners losses due to "atmospheric perils" (windstorm, hail, freezing)	For index: personal and/or commercial losses resulting from all catastrophic events For single events: personal and/or commercial losses resulting from "atmospheric" losses (wind, hail, snow, tropical storms, and hurricanes) or "earthquake" losses
•Possible Index Disaggregation	Zip code level data available for most areas	State/regional loss data
•Index Publication	Quarterly with a four-month lag Final index values about 12 months after the end of the loss period	Reported and updated daily Final index values available on the last business day of the 12th month following the end of the loss period

Sources: CBOT, IndexCo

CATEX: Risk for Cash and Risk for Risk

CATEX is essentially an electronic bulletin board on which insurance companies (CATEX subscribers) can list risks that they are eager to cede (under a traditional insurance treaty format) or to swap against other risks (reinsurance swap transaction). For instance, in a reinsurance swap transaction, an insurance company may decide to "swap" 10 units of New Jersey windstorm risk against 15 units of Ohio Valley tornado risk. A standard CATEX unit of risk is worth $1 million.

The CATEX trading system was built jointly by Science Applications International Corporation (SAIC), which designed the exchange's software, and Sun Microsystems, which provided the hardware. The rationale for the creation of an organized computer-based trading exchange is CATEX's belief that it will provide primary insurers with an efficient and therefore less costly management tool for risk distribution and diversification. In theory, there are fundamental reasons why a company may decide to assume or transfer exposure outside its area of expertise, among them the reduction of its concentration of risks in particular lines of business or geographic regions as well as the opportunity to adjust its risk profile in between annual renewal periods. In practice, one may wonder if a company could use the CATEX platform to unload its unwanted or residual risk to another company.

CATEX has not been technically designated as an exchange, but as a reinsurance intermediary by the New York Department of Insurance. Under New York law, CATEX cannot allow capital market firms, such as banks, dealers, hedge funds, or "transformer" firms, to access the system. Yet this restriction is bound to change, as CATEX, in a joint venture with the Bermuda Stock Exchange, plans to start operations in Bermuda. This offshore expansion will allow CATEX to include standardized reinsurance program offerings on its system as well as to welcome capital market players.

The current reinsurance intermediary status provides pros and cons for CATEX. On one hand, the ceding or the swapping of insurance risk is treated as traditional reinsurance, and existing insurance accounting practices can be used to record CATEX transactions. On the other, unlike entities such as the CBOT or the BCOE, which are designated as exchanges in their respective countries, CATEX does not benefit from the support of a clearing entity that would guarantee all transactions completed on its system. The resulting potential credit risk may not be a huge issue currently, as the insurance market is relatively soft, especially in the catastrophic risk area. There is no doubt, however, that clearing firms, as the ultimate guarantor of transactions, provide a sense of security to participating companies and members.

As of August 1998, CATEX had more than 50 subscribers and had facilitated over a dozen transactions through its system. CATEX had also penetrated the London market. Under an agreement with Lloyd's of London, CATEX offers a reduced subscription fee to members of Lloyd's.

Looking Ahead

Exchanges such as the Chicago Board of Trade, Bermuda Commodities Exchange, and Catastrophe Risk Exchange will undoubtedly play some role in the continued development of insurance derivatives and derivative-like structures. Two factors point the way: (1) exchanges' continued efforts to create and introduce "new and improved" insurance derivatives that combine established exchange market benefits, such as immediacy, price transparency, and clearing guarantees, with OTC-like customization and (2) insurers' and investors' increasing appetite for catastrophe bonds and other customized alternative risk transfer instruments. Traditionally, OTC markets have brought volume and liquidity to exchange markets, as OTC players look to lay off or adjust their position risk with plain-vanilla exchange-traded futures and options. Competitive pressures aside, the two markets often develop symbiotically.

The difficult hurdle facing exchange markets now, having garnered increasing insurer and investor acceptance, is liquidity. To be truly effective, exchange markets must attract broad, deep, and fairly continuous buying and selling. Yet potential market participants—the very buyers and sellers that can jump-start a market into maturity—typically wait to see such liquidity develop before entering the market in earnest. It's a Gordian knot that has dogged even some of today's most liquid markets in their early, developmental years. The exchange that finally cuts through this knot—whether through new product development or just by having the right infrastructure in place for the next market shock—may well create a truly continuous insurance mart for pricing, exchanging, and transferring insurance risk. When, where, and how that happens remains to be seen.

Second-Generation OTC Derivatives and Structured Products:
Catastrophe Bonds, Catastrophe Swaps, and Life Insurance Securitizations

Richard H. Bernero
Bankers Trust

We have now witnessed USAA's second year of using the capital markets to secure reinsurance capacity, irrespective of the continued softening of the insurance market. Japanese risks, both earthquake and wind, are being securitized too, whereas a year ago issuers primarily securitized U.S. risks alone. Securitization efforts have evolved into predictable lines of business, such as life insurance, allowing insurance companies to off-load mortality and expense fees and broadening the sources and types of risks for investors. Capital market products have evolved from "pilot studies" analyzed in strategic planning areas to the specialized domain of insurance companies' staffed derivative or structuring groups. Commercial and investment banks have entered the insurance sector, focusing on structuring and distribution capabilities, and established (re)insurance intermediary subsidiaries. Insurance companies, for their part, have expanded into the investment and commercial banking sector, and reinsurance intermediaries have established broker/dealer subsidiaries to underwrite and distribute securitization products.

Outside the insurance securitization arena, we have seen a similar blurring of lines, including:

• The application of over a dozen insurance companies for thrift charters to offer trust services or deposit-taking services nationally within the United States. Of these, approval is pending for AIG, Met Life, State Farm, Equitable, Allstate, the Hartford, Jackson National Life, Lumbersmen Mutual, SunAmerica, and Transamerica. Approval has been received by ReliaStar, Travelers, Principal Mutual, and Nationwide.

- The merger of Citibank and Travelers to form Citigroup, stretching the current boundaries of regulatory and financial reform. This action adds to the chain of events that have included the recently proposed financial reform bill H.R. 10; the 1916 National Bank Act allowing national banks in communities of 5,000 people or less to sell insurance; the 1986 Comptroller of the Currency ruling that federally chartered banks in small towns could sell insurance nationwide; amendments to the Bank Holding Act allowing bank holding companies in certain circumstances to engage in insurance activities; and grandfathering laws in such states as South Dakota and Delaware allowing bank holding companies to sell and underwrite insurance.

- The transformation of Lloyd's of London into a more "corporate" style of management and ownership, in part due to past liabilities but also in response to the increasingly competitive nature of the industry.

- The flow of sophisticated capital and resources to Bermuda, creating virtually overnight a large new source of risk capital. These companies have since expanded into the corporate-capital sector of Lloyd's, established beachheads in the United States, diversified outside property-catastrophe lines of business, and begun offering capital market solutions.

- The conversion of mutual insurance companies into stock-holding companies, in an effort to increase access to capital to fund growth and acquisitions and remain competitive.

- Regulatory acceptance for banks to use their own internal value-at-risk (VAR) systems to measure and monitor market risk for purposes of monitoring risk-based capital and calculating capital ratios.

Why is this happening? Deregulation, increasing competitive pressure, the globalization of business, innovation, and technological advances. Technology and financial services innovation and competition have redefined how we do business today. As this process continues, the evolution of derivatives as a risk management tool, and the application of securitization to new product lines, will further blur the distinction between banking and insurance.

Evolution

To explore this new area of financial engineering, it is important to have a brief sense of the history and evolution of the securitization, derivative, and structured note markets.

Securitization

Securitization emerged as a balance sheet tool in response to corporations', particularly mortgage lenders', evolving financial needs. With the growth in financial institutions extending credit to homeowners and issuing more mortgage loans, it became critical for them to effectively manage their balance sheets in a way that could make their limited capital efficiently support their growing loan portfolios. What emerged was the beginnings of the mortgage-backed securities market. It was, in effect, an effort to free up capital for mortgage lenders in a cost-effective manner. The effort took time, in part because, as with insurance, mortgages did not follow a consistent form or standard. But as time progressed, and as government organizations such the Federal Home Loan Bank and Federal Home Loan Mortgage Corporation (Freddie Mac) were set up, banks and mortgage banking lenders obtained the ability to issue mortgages, pool them, and then sell or assign them to these government agencies. The government agencies would in turn repackage the mortgages as securities by pooling the loans, breaking them down into various tranches that reflected distinct payment characteristics and expected maturities, and then issue these securities to the capital markets.

This technique of freeing up capital to support capital-intensive businesses similarly emerged in the credit sector. Today, it is very common for firms such as MBNA to securitize a pool of credit card receivables to cost-efficiently finance their credit card portfolios. Whereas the two main risks with mortgage-backed securities are interest rate and prepayment risk, with credit card receivables investors face interest rate risk (since outstanding balances are linked to some interest rate component) as well as the risk of delinquencies in payment by credit card holders. The fee that credit card firms pay to investors for assuming this risk is subsidized in part by the surcharges that the credit card companies receive on outstanding balances.

As the markets first became more comfortable with mortgage loans, and then subsequently with credit card receivables, corporations expanded the application of this concept of freeing up capital to other types of obligations. Soon the asset-backed securities market evolved, which pooled and securitized leases or obligations associated with underlying physical assets, such as equipment or car leases. Corporations discovered that they could securitize practically any asset for which they had a large portfolio that allowed for both some risk diversification and some homogeneity.

With the asset-backed securities market well established, using securitization to free up capital and/or monetize the value of various portfolios spread to other sectors. For example, cities and municipalities can now securitize anticipated future tax revenues (i.e., expectations of tax revenues to be paid over a forthcoming period of time) and sell these future tax revenues, in the form of securities, to investors in exchange for their assessed present value, minus any structuring fees and collateralization requirements. This allows a city or municipality to generate cash to cover budgetary needs or pay expenditures without having to be concerned about the timing of when it will actually receive the tax revenues.

As the securitization markets have evolved, and as investors have become more receptive to newer and different forms of risk, securitizations have moved from fairly predictable conforming pools of assets or liabilities to more esoteric or unique forms of risk. This evolution includes recent initiatives, albeit limited in scope and size, to securitize taxi medallion financing receivables and future royalties on an entertainer's work—so-called "Bowie bonds," named after rock star David Bowie, the first entertainer to have securitized his future royalties in order to monetize their present value.

All of the above described securitizations were capital or liquidity driven. They were ways to monetize assets or finance growth. Other more recent securitization initiatives, such as catastrophe bonds and residual value securitizations—in which equipment or auto lease finance companies pass on to investors all or a portion of the residual value of an asset at the end of a lease—go beyond monetization or financing needs. As with insurance, the motivation behind these securitizations is true risk transfer. The catastrophe bond investor assumes catastrophic insurance risk; the residual value investor assumes the risk that the residual value of an asset will not be as predicted. Such securitizations blur the traditional distinction between insurance and banking.

Derivatives

Although a relatively young discipline, derivatives have been around for some time now. As markets have become more dynamic, and people more sophisticated, so too have risk management needs and products evolved. Whereas derivatives were first used for risk management within the context of large financial institutions attempting to better manage the interest rate risk of their assets and liabilities, if you were to think about it, the world of derivatives has become an integral part of our daily lives. Credit cards can be chosen where finance charges are based on the opening, closing, or average balance for the billing period, and the designated finance fee may be a function of the prime rate plus a spread, a predetermined fixed rate, or the lesser of these two factors. Similarly, mortgages may be obtained in a variety of "flavors": 30-year fixed rate (conforming), 15-year fixed rate (conforming), 6-month Libor ARM, 1-year convertible ARM, 3-year/6-month convertible ARM, 5/1 ARM, 7/1 ARM, 5-year fixed-rate balloon, 7-year fixed-rate balloon. These common-day consumer products—credit cards and mortgage loans—are, in effect, derivative-linked loans, in that our liability is linked to a particular index or rate. We are, in effect, choosing a particular product whereby the "derivative" component matches our particular risk appetite, cost constraints, and liquidity needs.

Broadly speaking, the derivatives markets are usually broken down into three classes of products: futures, options, and swaps. Futures and options are the oldest form of derivatives, whereas swaps are a relatively recent phenomenon. The first currency swap was engineered in London in 1979, with the first major visible deal transacted in 1981. This landmark swap, involving the World Bank and IBM, set the stage for future developments. The World Bank wanted to obtain Swiss francs (CHF) and Deutsche marks (DEM), but had already issued a fair amount of debt in Switzerland and Germany. At the same time, IBM wanted to recognize FX gains on a portion of its existing CHF and DEM bonds. By working through a third-party financial institution, these two parties were able to meet their objectives with offsetting currency swaps. Interest rate swaps were the next major derivative product development to follow, in 1981, with the first significant transaction coming one year later. The first visible deal for interest rate risk involved the Student Loan Marketing Association (Sallie Mae), which entered into a fixed-for-floating interest rate swap to better manage and convert the interest rate characteristics of its liabilities.

Just as mortgages have developed a variety of flavors, so too have swaps increased in number and variety as the markets have developed and corporate needs expanded:

- fixed-for-floating swaps (basic or plain-vanilla swaps)
- zero-coupon-for-floating swaps
- basis swaps (floating-for-floating swaps)
- callable swaps
- putable swaps
- extendable swaps
- forward-starting swaps (deferred swaps)
- deferred rate-setting swaps
- rate-capped swaps (mini-max, barrier, knock-in, and knock-out swaps)
- amortizing swaps
- asset-based swaps (total return swaps)

Structured Notes

Structured notes, which are generally defined as fixed-income securities linked to derivatives (see figure 3-1), were created in 1985. For issuers, structured notes provide a vehicle to raise capital at a lower cost than they could by issuing fixed-rate notes. For investors, structured notes provide a more attractive risk/reward profile than conventional securities. Structured notes come in a variety of flavors, including:

- floating rate notes (capped and inverse floaters)
- CMT/CMS floating rate notes (CMT-Libor differential notes)
- Prime-Libor differential notes
- accrual notes, range notes, and index amortizing notes
- commodity-linked notes
- quanto/currency-linked notes
- total return index notes

Figure 3-1 Derivative, Securitization, and Structured Note Flow of Funds

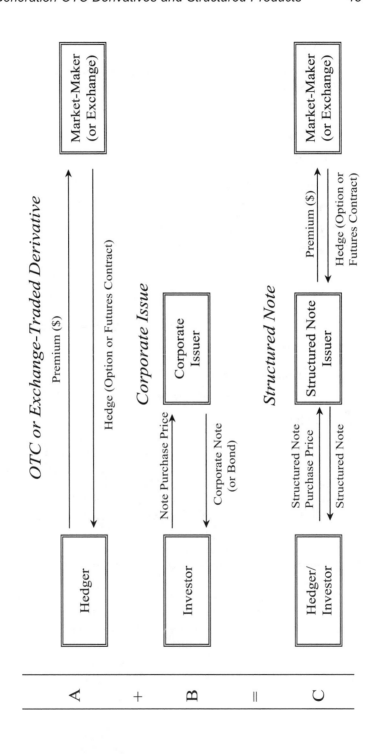

Drivers

What were the drivers that led to these landmark transactions and that precipitated the continued and growing use of derivatives by corporations to this date? They include:

- price volatility
- the globalization of the financial markets
- tax asymmetries
- regulatory changes and increasing competition
- the decreasing cost of information and transactions
- liquidity needs
- risk aversion
- accounting benefits

In effect, derivatives have become a means to accomplish one or more of the following:

- risk management ("hedging")
- balance sheet management
- capital management

There are three different, but related, ways to manage financial risks. The first is to purchase insurance. Insurance, however, is only viable for the management of certain types of financial risks. Such risks are said to be insurable. The second approach is asset/liability management. This approach involves the careful balancing of assets and liabilities so as to eliminate net value changes. Asset/liability management is most often used in the management of interest rate risk and exchange rate risk. The final approach, which can be used either by itself or in conjunction with one or both of the other two, is hedging. Hedging involves taking offsetting risk positions. It is very similar to asset/liability management, but while asset/liability management, by definition, involves on-balance sheet positions, hedging usually involves off-balance sheet positions, namely, derivatives. This distinction between asset/liability management and hedging is important but often overlooked. The objectives behind a corporation's use of derivatives to hedge liabilities, or even to fund new assets, can include:

- hedging price risk
- lowering financing costs
- operating on a larger scale
- gaining access to new markets

Within the context of asset/liability management, risk-reducing activities such as insurance and hedging can assist in creating contingent capital, in that a small premium is paid for the right to tap potential capital above a certain threshold or loss amount. Debt and equity are more direct sources of capital. Depending on the balance of debt, equity, and reinsurance/hedging activities chosen, the source, permanence, and cost of capital will vary (see figure 3-2 on page 48). Equity capital is the most direct form of capital. By issuing equity, a company transfers all of its general risks to shareholders in exchange for some of the upside potential of the firm. Debt is a more cost-effective, contingent source of capital versus equity, in that a company agrees to pay a risk premium for a period of time in exchange for the right to borrow capital and repay it by some finite date. Reinsurance/hedging may be even more cost-effective, albeit more contingent in nature.

Derivatives' ability to provide alternative capital—and possibly to lower capital financing cost—explains much of the current drive to apply securitization, derivative, and structured product technologies to insurance-related risks. Although the initial convergence of banking and insurance was driven by a lack of capacity in the insurance markets, insurance companies now want to expand their use of capital market products for *strategic* reasons. They are driven by a desire to tap alternative sources of capital, as well as flexible alternative sources of liquidity, as consolidation reduces the number of (re)insurance companies. They also see the securitization/derivatization of insurance risks as a potential way to cut costs, optimize their portfolios, and redeploy their capital into new risk management products. In the early days, a premium has been required to broaden the base of risk takers, but as investors become more comfortable with these types of risks, tapping the capital markets may become a more cost-efficient alternative for the insurance industry.

Figure 3-2 Balancing Capital's Cost and Contingent Nature

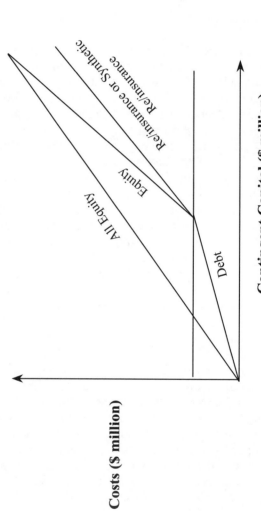

Insurance-Linked Securitization and Derivative Products

As we have discussed, over the last few years we have witnessed a series of new derivative and securitization initiatives to tackle new risks and package new assets. These second-generation structured notes, swaps, and securities apply existing capital market structuring expertise to create a potential new set of asset classes for investors, leading to new risk and capital management tools for corporations.

During the course of the subsequent pages, we will endeavor to shed some light on the application of securitization and derivative technologies to address liability-based scenarios in the emerging property-catastrophe and life insurance securitization and derivative markets. Although this chapter and this book focus primarily on the securitization/derivatization of insurance risks within the context of property-catastrophe risk, we cannot overlook that derivatives are also offered within a variety of life insurance-related products: equity-indexed annuities, guaranteed minimum income benefit (GMIB) products, and variable annuities with guaranteed minimum death benefit (GMDB) features, to name a few. Amongst the tools we will briefly describe and analyze here are:

- catastrophe bonds
- catastrophe swaps
- mortality & expense (M&E) fee / life insurance acquisition cost securitizations

Note that derivative and securitization developments in these liability-based insurance areas parallel emerging innovations in credit securitization, including collateralized loan and bond obligations. With such structures, banks have securitized portions of their loan portfolios, effectively selling them and removing them from their balance sheets. Innovations like these have been driven by the narrowing of spreads for loans kept on books and by increasing pressure on capital ratios, which has led companies to pursue new ways to cost-effectively service clients while reducing their own risk exposure.

Catastrophe Bonds

Over the last ten or so years, we have seen dramatic changes in the insurance industry, many precipitated by the occurrence of large catastrophic events such as Hurricane Hugo in 1989, Hurricane Andrew in 1992, and the Northridge earthquake near Los Angeles in 1993. These events had dramatic repercussions in the insurance industry, catching some companies by surprise. For example, one reinsurer lost a third to a half of its capital and surplus on Hurricane Andrew alone. Although the insurance industry is by nature a risk-taking one, the size of these events was above anything that had ever been contemplated by some companies. Further, Hurricane Andrew, albeit very significant in size and causing major damage, by no means reached its full destructive potential, hitting nearby Homestead as opposed to Miami. If Andrew had hit Miami, estimates suggest insured losses of at least $50-100 billion.

These events caused the industry to revisit how it has analyzed and modeled such risk. Insurers and reinsurers had already put significant effort into assessing risks, but they now faced additional pressure from shareholders and rating agencies. Rating agencies, in particular, put additional onus on insurance companies to quantify and represent their exposures to 1-in-100-year scenarios like Andrew. Such pressures led to increased company focus on quantifying extreme catastrophic risk and fostered the market for the services of various catastrophe modeling firms, including Risk Management Solutions (RMS), Applied Insurance Research (AIR), EQE International (EQE), and modeling firms owned by other consulting or actuarial firms.

The succession of catastrophic events also led to a shift in pricing. The market had been hardening already. Yet these events put greater upward pressure on reinsurance pricing. Companies looking to hedge their risk were hitting obstacles, both in terms of concerns over the credit quality of the companies they were buying reinsurance from (who may have incurred substantial losses from Hurricane Andrew or other events) and in terms of concerns over their ability to buy protection at affordable prices. Such changes in market dynamics led to the infusion of capital in Bermuda to set up new companies—really the first foray by capital market investors to capitalize insurance risk. The changes also led to the development of catastrophe bonds and contingent financing alternatives to insurance, both as a means to obtain collateralized or good creditworthy reinsurance alternatives as well as to buy protection at a size that could not be bought in the reinsurance market (or at least not at a cost the client was willing to pay).

As figure 3-3 on page 52 shows, the generic flow of a catastrophe bond is to take the premium from a client buying reinsurance, plus the collateralization of risk exposure, that is, the proceeds from the investors, and to pool these two cash flows in a special purpose vehicle (SPV), which earns income ideally on a tax-free or tax-deferred basis and which basically serves as a fully collateralized source of recovery for the client. In the early days, insurance clients had two priorities: to buy protection, but also to have that protection treated like other reinsurance, that is, to get the appropriate accounting treatment. This dual goal necessitated the use of an SPV or transformer company that would allow the client or cedent to enter into a reinsurance contract. The SPV's sole purpose was to write the reinsurance contract and then proceed to issue securities linked to it. The SPV/transformer structure catered to investors too, who could not enter into reinsurance contracts directly and who preferred to make "investments," ideally in the form of purchasing a rated security. As the market has evolved, insurance companies have shown a greater willingness to look at derivative tools and techniques, such as swaps, that do not use SPVs or provide reinsurance accounting treatment.

In general, catastrophe bonds fall into three main types (see table 3-1 on pages 53-58 for a detailed listing). First, many deals are associated with a single peril, such as a single large hurricane or earthquake incurred by a company (e.g., USAA or Tokio Marine & Fire). Second, other deals have been done on a basket or portfolio basis, whereby the client is looking to hedge or protect multiple risks, such as in the deals done for Hannover Re, St. Paul Re (through Georgetown Re) and F&G Re (through Mosaic Re). Last, some deals pertain to single perils, but rather than covering company-specific exposure, they are triggered by an index such as PCS. Notable examples include Swiss Re (via SR Earthquake Fund) and Reliance National (via SLF Re).

The first catastrophe bond deals focused, by and large, on obtaining risk transfer for extreme catastrophic events. Most deals tended to have an exceedence probability (EP) or risk trigger linked to something close to a 1-in-100-year type of event. Given the fact that buyers in the capital markets had never looked at such risk before, the first stage of the insurance securitization process was to match buyers and sellers—to find investors willing to assume insurance risk. Underwriters quickly discovered that rating the deal by a rating agency such as Standard & Poor's or Moody's was critical, or at least a very positive enhancement, because such ratings allowed investors the means to attempt to compare the risk against a traditional credit benchmark.

The early deals tended to be divided into two tranches to cater to different investor classes: a AAA tranche and a lower-rated tranche, usually in the BB range. Both from the insurance company's and investment bank's perspectives, the goal was to broaden the distribution base as much as possible. Having at least two tranches acknowledged the fact that different investor classes have different market criteria for what they can

Figure 3-3 Catastrophe Bond Flow of Funds

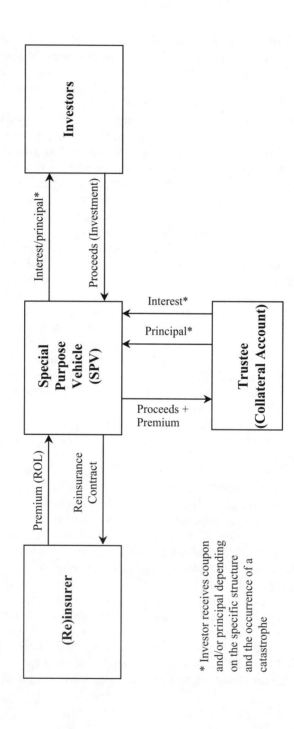

* Investor receives coupon and/or principal depending on the specific structure and the occurrence of a catastrophe

Table 3-1 Property-Catastrophe Deals

Synthetic Reinsurance: Catastrophe Bonds, Catastrophe Swaps, and Other Risk Transfer Structures

Insurance Company or Agent (Vehicle Name)	Amount and Rating (S&P/Moody/Fitch/Duff)	Type of Instrument	Issue Date	Maturity	Description
Hannover Re I	$85 million [NR/NR/NR/NR]	Portfolio-linked swap/note	1995		$85 mm risk transfer.
Phoenix Re/AIG (through Benfield Ellinger)	$10 million (L+795 bp) [NR/NR/NR/NR]	Catastrophe-linked bonds	Apr. 1996	2-year program (1 year risk, 1 year reporting)	Catastrophe losses in any of five geographic areas exceeding pre-set levels. $10 mm risk transfer.
Hannover Re II (K2)	$100 million [NR/NR/NR/NR]	Portfolio-linked swap	Nov. 1996	5-year program, optional 2-year extension	Company performance on exposures in U.S., Japan, and Europe as well as aviation. Trigger 100% combined ratio. $100 mm risk transfer.
St. Paul Companies (Georgetown Re)	$68.5 million, as follows: -$44.5 million notes (6.097%) [AAA/Aaa/NA/NR] -$24 million preference shares (14.15%) [NR/NR/NR/NR]	Loss-linked notes and preference shares	Dec. 1996	Notes: 2007 Shares: 2000	Investors' returns linked to company performance. $45.2 mm risk transfer.
Reliance National I (SLF Reinsurance Ltd.)	$20–40 million proposed ($10 million issued) (L+812 bp) [NR/NR/NR/NR]	Catastrophe-linked bonds	Mar. 1997	18-month program (6/30/98)	Company performance on five classes of insurance risk (U.S. property, ROW property, space launch, aviation, marine) for 1-year period. $10 mm risk transfer.
USAA I (Residential Re)	$476.98 million, as follows: -$163.8 million class A-1 (1mL+273 bp) [AAAr/Aaa/AAA/AAA] -$313.18 million class A-2 (1mL+576 bp) [BB/Ba2/BBB/BB]	Catastrophe-linked bonds	Jun. 1997	6/98 if no loss; 12/98 if loss; principal protected notes extendible	At risk due to single hurricane causing in excess of $1 billion of insured losses to USAA. 0.7% EP. $400 mm risk transfer.
Reinsurer—undisclosed	$35 million (L+519 bp) [NR/NR/NR/NR]	Catastrophe-linked swap	Jul. 1997	11 months	Index-based swap linked to USAA/Res Re deal. 0.7% EP. $35 mm risk transfer.

Table 3-1 Property-Catastrophe Deals, *con't.*

Insurance Company or Agent (Vehicle Name)	Amount and Rating (S&P/Moody/Fitch/Duff)	Type of Instrument	Issue Date	Maturity	Description
Swiss Re (SR Earthquake Fund)	$137 million, as follows: -$42 million class A-1 (3mL+255 bp) -$20 million class A-2 (8.645% quarterly) [NR/Baa3/NA/NR] -$60.3 million class B (10.493%/T+475 bp/L+445 bp quarterly) [NR/Ba1/NA/NR] -$14.7 million class C (11.952%/T+675 bp quarterly)	Catastrophe-linked bonds	Jul. 1997	24-month program	At risk due to single earthquake in California causing in excess of $12 billion of insured losses to the industry. Partial principal write-down for A-1, A-2, and B classes begins at $18.5 billion loss, with full loss at $24 billion. EP of 0.41%, 0.41%, 0.68%, and approximately 1% for A-1, A-2, B, and C respectively. $112.2 mm risk transfer.
Tokio Fire & Marine (Parametric Re)	$100 million, as follows: -$80 million FRN (6mL+430 bp) [NR/Ba2/NA/BB] -$20 million units (6mL+206 bp) [NR/Baa3/NA/BBB-]	Catastrophe-linked bonds	Dec. 1997	10-year maturity (1-year risk period)	At risk due to single earthquake in Japan of 7.1 or greater magnitude. 0.7% EP. $90 mm risk transfer.
Reliance National II (SLF Reinsurance Ltd.)	$20–40 million proposed ($20 million issued) (L+925 bp) [NR/NR/NR/NR]	Catastrophe-linked bonds	Jan. 1998	18-month program	Company performance on five classes of insurance risk (U.S. property, ROW property, space launch, aviation, marine) for 1-year period. 11.06% EP
Florida Select Insurance	$83.569 million, as follows: -$22.036 million class A-1 (10-year partially principal protected notes) (L+182 bp) [NR/Aaa/AAA/NR] -$61.533 million class A-2 (principal at risk) (L+436 bp) [NR/Ba3/BB/NR]	Catastrophe-linked bonds	Mar. 1998	Notes: 1 year, extendible to 10 years Shares: 10 months Risk period 0.83 year (12/31/98)	Hurricane risk in western Florida on policies company purchased from Florida JUA. 0.83% EP. $72 mm risk transfer.
Mitsui Marine & Fire	$30 million (L+375 bp) [NR/NR/NR/NR]	Catastrophe-linked swap	Apr. 1998	3-year program (4/01)	Direct issuance of earthquake-linked swap based on magnitude of earthquakes of at least 7.1 in and around Tokyo region. 0.7% EP. $30 mm risk transfer.

Table 3-1 Property-Catastrophe Deals, *con't.*

Insurance Company or Agent (Vehicle Name)	Amount and Rating (S&P/Moody/Fitch/Duff)	Type of Instrument	Issue Date	Maturity	Description
Reliance National III (SLF Reinsurance Ltd.)	$? million (L+837.5 bp, if issued) 1.5% option premium per year [NR/NR/NR/NR]	Catastrophe-linked bonds (insurance-linked optionable note)	May 1998	3-year program	Linked to company performance on five risk classes (U.S. property, WWex U.S. property, aviation, marine drilling rigs, satellite launch failure).
CNA/Continental Casualty Company (HF Re Ltd.)	$50 million (6mT+375 bp indicative) [NR/NR/NR/NR]	Catastrophe-linked bonds	Jun. 1998	12/17/98 if no loss, 12/9/99 if extended	Northeast U.S. hurricane risk, attaching at $10 billion PCS, exhausting at $15 billion PCS. 1.318% EP; 0.979% expected loss. $50 mm risk transfer.
Yasuda Fire & Marine (Pacific Re)	$80 million (3mL+370 bp) / 3mL+950 bp (3mL+950 bp if drop-down event) [NR/Ba3/BB/NR]	Catastrophe-linked bonds	Jun. 1998	5-year program	Japanese wind-related risk. Attachment point of 0.94% EP, as calculated by RMS. Top-and-drop concept whereby if losses exceed 3.35% annual EP, converts to 2nd event cover on a loss with a 5.12% loss EP.
USAA II (Residential Re)	$450 million FRN (3mL+416 bp) [BB/Ba2/BB/BB]	Catastrophe-linked bonds	Jun. 1998	6/1/99 if no loss, 12/99 if loss; principal protected notes extendible	At risk due to single hurricane (category 3 or greater) causing in excess of $1 billion of insured losses to USAA; some coupon risk.
U.S. insurer—undisclosed	$? million (L+500 bp) [NR/NR/NR/NR]	Catastrophe-linked option	Jul. 1998	1-year program	Trigger based on a major earthquake in California causing insured property losses greater than the strike of the option. Investors received substantial upfront premium, but must pay a percentage of losses above the strike. EP 2.0%.
F&G Re (Mosaic Re)	$60 million, as follows: -$18 million class A units (L+216.5 bp) [NR/NR/NR/AAA] -$21 million class B notes (L+827 bp) [NR/NR/NR/B] -$15 million class A notes (L+444 bp) [NR/NR/NR/BB]	Catastrophe-linked bonds	Jul. 1998	1-year program (7/1/99)	Provides retrocessional coverage on an aggregate excess-of-loss basis for a defined portfolio of U.S. catastrophe excess-of-loss reinsurance contracts. EP 0.61% for class A units and notes, 2.75% for class B notes. $54 mm risk transfer.

Table 3-1 Property-Catastrophe Deals, *con't.*

Insurance Company or Agent (Vehicle Name)	Amount and Rating (S&P/Moody/Fitch/Duff)	Type of Instrument	Issue Date	Maturity	Description
X.L. Mid-Ocean Re	$200 million, as follows: -$45 million tranche A (3mL+404 bp) [NR/NR/NR/NR] -$55 million tranche B (3mL+578 bp) [NR/NR/NR/NR]	Catastrophe-linked swap	Jul. 1998	8/99 if no loss, 2/01 if loss and extended	Covers the upper layers of X.L. Mid-Ocean's hurricane and earthquake exposure in the U.S. and its territories and possessions in the Caribbean.
N.Y. reinsurer—undisclosed	$10 million	"Basis swap" reinsurance	Aug. 1998	1-year program (8/22/99)	Payouts linked to the comparative movements of industry losses as calculated by PCS against actual windstorm losses incurred by the unnamed reinsurer. Losses pertain to those incurred in all U.S. states touching the Atlantic Ocean or the Gulf of Mexico.
U.S. insurer—undisclosed (via SG Acceptance NV)	$25 million (3mL+160-75 bp) (190 bp upfront if in option form)	Catastrophe-linked bonds or options	Oct. 1998	11/15/99 if no loss, 10/31/00 if less than $3 billion, 10/31/01 if $3-10 billion (1-year risk period)	New Madrid (U.S. Midwest) earthquake risk, attaching at $8 billion PCS, with full loss of principal at $10 billion PCS. 0.75% EP per RMS.

Contingent Surplus Notes Insurance Company or Agent (Vehicle Name)	Amount and Rating (S&P/Moody/Fitch/Duff)	Type of Instrument	Issue Date	Maturity	Description
Nationwide Mutual Insurance (Nationwide CSN Trust)	$400 million, as follows: -$392 million senior notes (9.875%) -$8 million junior notes (12.22%)	Contingent surplus notes	Feb. 1995	2025, callable thereafter	Trust purchases Treasuries due in 2005; required to deliver Treasuries to Nationwide in exchange for Nationwide surplus.
Arkwright Mutual Insurance Company (Arkwright CSN Trust)	$100 million trust notes (9.625%) [BBB/Baa3/NR/A] $2 million trust certificates (9.625%)	Contingent surplus notes	May 1996	2026, callable through 2016	Arkwright may exchange its surplus notes for Treasuries held by the trust. Trust certificates subordinated to trust notes.

Table 3-1 Property-Catastrophe Deals, *con't.*

Other Non-life Structures

Insurance Company or Agent (Vehicle Name)	Amount and Rating (S&P/Moody/Fitch/Duff)	Type of Instrument	Issue Date	Maturity	Description
RLI Corp.	$50 million	Catastrophe equity puts	Oct. 1996	3-year program	RLI can put up to $50 million of convertible preferred shares to Centre Re at a pre-negotiated rate if there is a catastrophe.
Winterthur Insurance	$290 million	Catastrophe convertible bonds	Jan. 1997	Jan. 2000	Three-year convertible bonds, coupon of 2.25% not paid if automobile claims exceed a threshold level. $6.3 mm risk transfer.
Horace Mann	$100 million	Catastrophe equity puts	Mar. 1997	3-year program, extendible to five	Horace Mann can put up to $100 million of convertible preferred shares to Centre Re at a pre-negotiated rate if there are one or more catastrophes exceeding $65 million in aggregate.
Lasalle Re	$100 million	Catastrophe equity puts	Jul. 1997	Multi-year	Lasalle Re can put up to $100 million of convertible preferred shares to participants at a pre-negotiated rate if there are one or more qualifying catastrophes.
Toyota Motors Credit Corp. (Gramercy Place Ltd.)	$566.28 million, as follows: $60.68 million class A FRN (3mL+23 bp) [AA/Aa2/NR/NR] $283.13 million class B FRN (3mL+45 bp) [A/A2/NR/NR] $122.47 million class C-1 FRN (3mL+325 bp) [BB/Ba2/NR/NR] $100 million class C-2 notes (8.95%) [BB/Ba2/NR/NR]	Residual value securitization			Residual value risk on resale value of 260,000 leased Toyota vehicles. AA notes: one-year notes, at risk if sales prices fall more than 23% below expectations. A notes: two-year notes, at risk if sales prices fall more than 15% below expectations. BB notes: three-year average life, principal at risk if sales prices fall more than 9% below issuer's expectations.

Table 3-1 Property-Catastrophe Deals, *con't.*

Withdrawn/Canceled Deals

Insurance Company or Agent (Vehicle Name)	Amount and Rating (S&P/Moody/Fitch/Duff)	Type of Instrument	Issue Date	Maturity	Description
AIG	$100 million	Catastrophe-linked bonds	1992		Bond to replicate AIG's reinsurance program, with coupon payments triggered by an index of PCS and AM Best data created by AIG once loss ratio exceeds a certain threshold.
Normandy Re	$25 million	Catastrophe-linked bonds	Before 1995	3-year program	3-year maturity, triggered by PCS index. 1% probability of attachment.
USAA	$100 million	Catastrophe-linked bonds	1996		
Cat Limited	$50 million (T+450 bp)	Catastrophe-linked bonds	1996	5-month program	UNL trigger. 1.1% probability of attachment.
ACE Limited	$35-45 million (L+550 bp)	Catastrophe-linked bonds	1996	14-month program	PCS index. 2% probability of attachment.
California Earthquake Authority (CEA)	$3,500 million (L+1075 bp)	Catastrophe-linked bonds	1995/96	10-year program	Interest payments at risk due to earthquake. 1.27% probability of attachment. $1.5 billion risk transfer
Bermuda reinsurer— undisclosed	$300-350 million (tentatively rated A2)	Catastrophe-linked bonds	1997	3-year program	Trigger based on up to 3 separate $12.5 billion or greater industry losses in the U.S.

Sources: Goldman Sachs, Guy Carpenter, Sedgwick Lane Financial, and company press releases. While the information contained in this report was obtained from sources believed to be reliable, no guarantee can be made as to its accuracy or completeness.

and cannot invest in. Most institutional investors are subject to certain investment guidelines, which reference, amongst other things, rating criteria, target return, or spread above a certain investment benchmark. Pension companies and money managers, for example, might require AA or better as their minimum credit to invest in a deal. Other investors, such as hedge funds, emerging market funds, or other private placement investors, may be more receptive to lower-rated deals because of the incremental yield produced.

For example, consider the June 1997 USAA deal, one of the first and largest catastrophe bond forays into the capital markets. To cater to different investor classes, the risk was broken into two tranches: one rated AAA, the other BB. The AAA securities were collateralized, as a portion of the proceeds from the notes was used to buy government securities as collateral to guarantee principal protection at maturity (a prerequisite for a AAA rating). Specifically, of the $163.8 million of the AAA notes issued, roughly 50% was used to buy 10-year zero-coupon Treasuries, which cost about 50 cents on the dollar. Maturing at par (100 cents on the dollar), the 10-year Treasury notes serve to cover the entire principal. Note that because of this collateralization, only 50% of the AAA issuance was true risk transfer. The deal's pricing reflects this: the pricing of the AAA notes was half the spread of the BB notes—273 vs. 576 basis points (bp) over Libor.

As figures 3-4a through 3-4d on pages 60-61 reflect, the nature of the risk each securitization represents also affects the type of investor classes that participate. For example, in the USAA deal, money managers and mutual funds represented more than 50% of the investor base. For the St. Paul/Georgetown Re deal, on the other hand, the money manager/mutual fund component was extremely small, reflecting the different nature of the risk. Here the deal was based on a more-difficult-to-model portfolio of risk, whereas USAA represented the single-company risk of a well-known firm. Further, the preference shares were unrated. Life insurers and hedge funds took up the slack left by the mutual funds and money managers. Historically, life insurance companies have been large investors in lower-rated and private placement transactions. Because their liabilities are long-dated, and more predictable, they tend to invest in real estate and other assets whose value might be more uncertain but that, over a long period of time, produce attractive returns.

Figure 3-4a Risk Capital by Investor Class
St. Paul Re/Georgetown Re

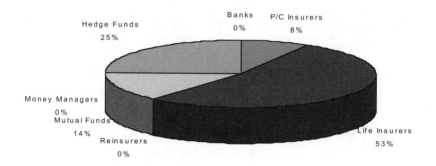

Risk Capital (%) - St. Paul Re (Georgetown Re)

Figure 3-4b Risk Capital by Investor Class
USAA/Residential Re

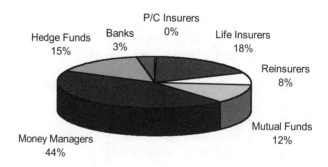

Risk Capital (%) - USAA (Residential Re)

Figure 3-4c Risk Capital by Investor Class
Swiss Re/SR Earthquake Fund

Risk Capital (%) - Swiss Re (SR Earthquake Fund))

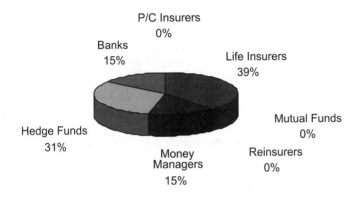

Figure 3-4d Risk Capital by Investor Class
Tokio M&F/Pacific Re

Risk Capital (%) - Tokio M&F (Pacific Re)

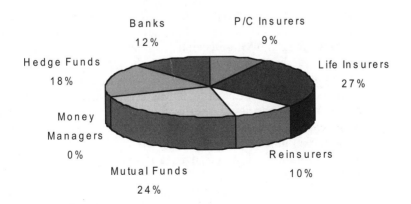

Catastrophe Swaps

As the market for insurance risk has developed, insurance companies and investors have become more comfortable with derivative deals, particularly swaps, which closely replicate traditional reinsurance (see figure 3-5). More and more, we are witnessing the use of derivative technology as a considered alternative to catastrophe bond structures. In fact, a recent transaction involving Swiss Re actually applied swap derivative technology while keeping the risk transfer in traditional reinsurance form, creating "basis swap" reinsurance. Note that due to the costs associated with larger deals and issuing securities, the catastrophe swap market is more receptive to smaller size deals. Most swap deals to date have been done on the order of $100 million or less. Swap deals can also be executed on a more timely basis.

The most notable, most recent examples of using swaps to address catastrophe risk include a swap done by Mitsui in April 1998 and a swap done by X.L. Mid-Ocean in July 1998. In many ways, the Mitsui swap represents the same type of exposure that Tokio F&M had done in the form of a security issued by Parametric Re in December 1997, with cover triggered by a Japanese earthquake of a magnitude of at least 7.1 on the Richter scale. Yet rather than get a reinsurance contract from an SPV, which in turn would issue securities to investors, Mitsui entered into a transaction with Swiss Re, which assumed the risk, perhaps in the form of reinsurance, on its own balance sheet. Swiss Re then laid off the risk to investors in swap form.

More recently, in the form of an actual direct issuance, X.L. Mid-Ocean entered into a swap transaction with a series of investors. In this case, X.L. actually marketed its risk to three markets—the traditional reinsurance market, the alternative risk transfer or financial reinsurance market, and the capital markets—with the goal of placing up to $200 million of risk. Since X.L. and Mid-Ocean had agreed to merge, entering into this transaction gave both companies a timely hedge for the aggregation of the two companies' risk during the merger transition period. Further, due to the merger's imminent closing, it was critical that the transaction be done as quickly as possible, especially in light of it being in the middle of the hurricane season. In the end, the financial reinsurance market and the swap market quickly delivered risk capital to X.L. Roughly $90-100 million of insurance risk was transferred in swap form to a series of capital market investors.

Swiss Re's "basis swap" reinsurance transaction, as mentioned, applied these derivative concepts, but did so while not actually employing a derivative structure. A basis swap is a swap linked to the exchange

Figure 3-5 Catastrophe Swap Flow of Funds

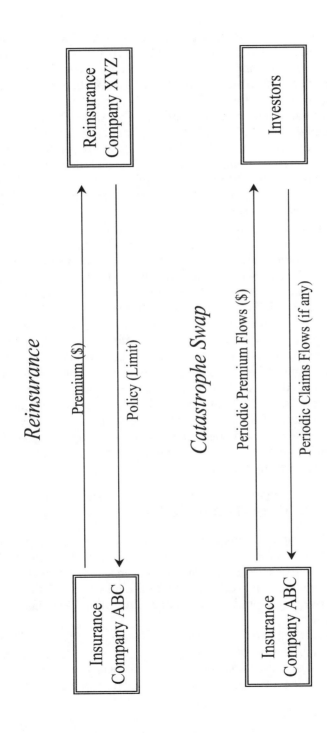

between two different indices (see figure 3-6). For example, one of the more common ones in the fixed-income derivatives market is the basis swap between Libor and commercial paper (as opposed a normal interest rate swap such as fixed-for-floating: paying a fixed coupon vs. receiving a floating rate such as Libor). The Swiss Re transaction involved two separate reinsurance contracts to replicate this structure: one paying an exchange of premiums for the companies' performance, the other paying an exchange of premiums for an industry index. If you net the two contracts (assuming the premiums were roughly the same), what you really have is a basis swap, where one company is paying for when its company-specific losses exceed the index and the other company is paying for when the index exceeds its losses.

Insurance companies' receptivity toward derivative technology has increased as capital market deals find successful placement. Other derivative and structured products, such as options, contingent surplus notes, and catastrophe equity puts (CatEPuts), have also found use as risk transfer and risk financing vehicles (see figure 3-7 on page 66 for the spectrum of risk transfer/risk financing products and table 3-1 for specific examples). It would not be at all surprising to see an increasing use of derivative concepts in addressing catastrophic insurance risk to complement or balance securitization issues. In fact, the most recent deal, linked to New Madrid earthquake risk, was offered both in note and option form to reflect receptivity toward multiple structures. Just as catastrophe bond investors come from different sectors of the investment spectrum depending on the nature of the risk, so too may certain investor classes have a preference for certain structures. Some may prefer option or swap forms, whereas other investor classes may not be able to do derivatives or may simply prefer security forms.

Mortality & Expense (M&E) Fee / Life Insurance Acquisition Cost Securitizations

Although the nature of this chapter and this book is to focus on the property-catastrophe side of the insurance business, we cannot overlook the life side. First, because securitization has been active in that area. Second, because down the road, securitization of life insurance liabilities, such as mortality risk, could produce yet another alternative asset class or type of risk for investors.

As mentioned before, in most cases, excepting catastrophe bonds and residual value securitizations, the primary impetus behind securitization is to free up the capital constraints of the balance sheet, providing liquidity or cash flows by laying off liabilities or monetizing future revenue.

Figure 3-6 Catastrophe "Basis Swap" Reinsurance Flow of Funds

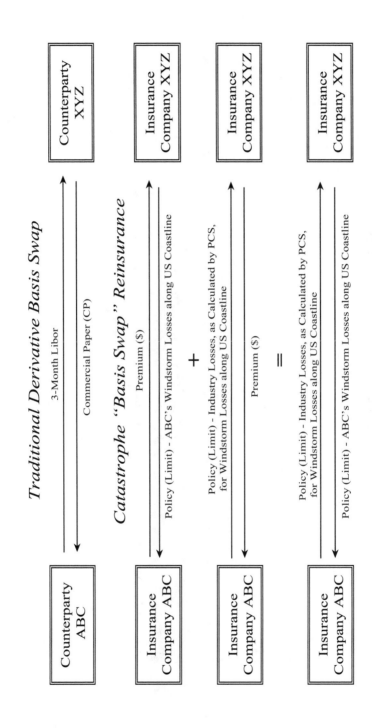

Figure 3-7 Risk Transfer/Risk Financing Spectrum

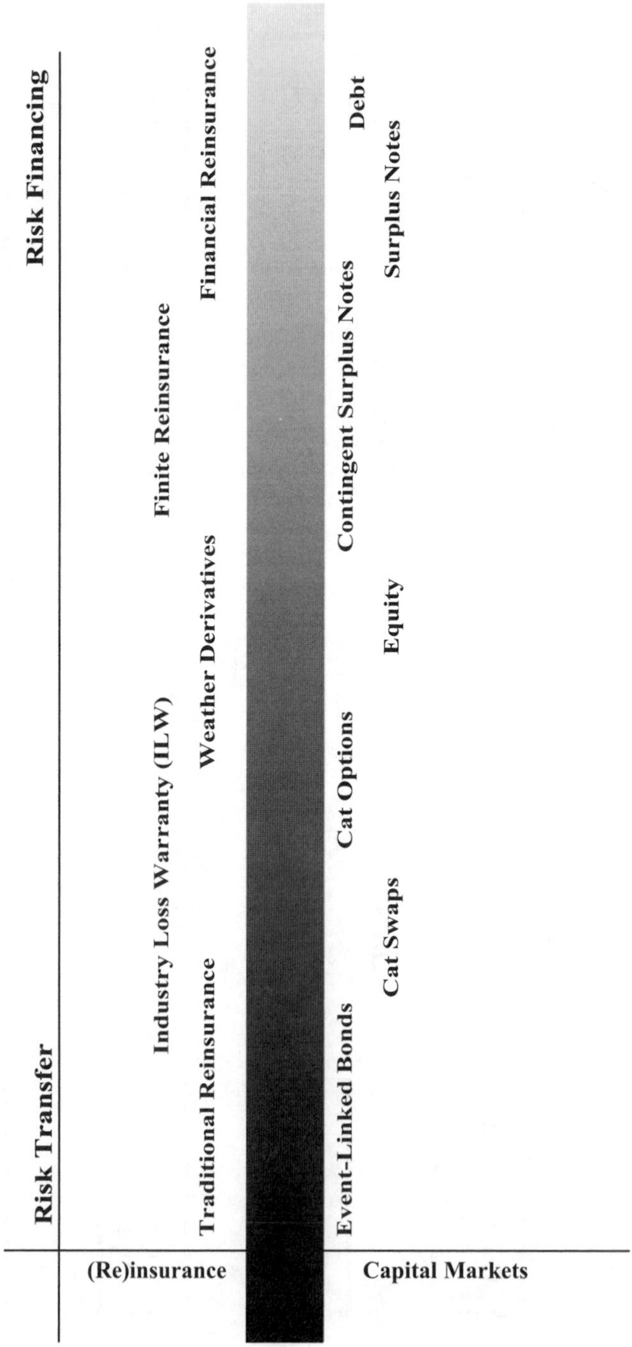

Risk Transfer

Risk Financing

Traditional Reinsurance

Industry Loss Warranty (ILW)

Weather Derivatives

Finite Reinsurance

Financial Reinsurance

Event-Linked Bonds

Cat Swaps

Cat Options

Equity

Contingent Surplus Notes

Surplus Notes

Debt

(Re)insurance   Capital Markets

The early stages of life insurance securitization have followed this traditional model and focused on providing capital or cash. Specifically, in the deals detailed below, the primary motive was to help finance a cash strain that life insurers incur with their mortality and expense fees and their acquisition costs. In effect, every time a life company sells a life policy or variable annuity, a potentially significant portion of the cash flows received in the first year are used to pay the distributor, broker, or agent who sourced the transaction. Insurance companies pay out these fees at inception, but only get the cash flows back over time. Usually, insurers have to amortize the cost over a three-to-five-year period.

That creates a balance sheet constraint on growth, just like in the credit card sector, where companies have limited capital to pay all the balances owing on credit card purchases while they wait for the cash to come in. Three recent securitizations freed up those capital constraints for the growing life business (see table 3-2 on pages 68-69). In each case—whether American Skandia in the United States, National Providence in the United Kingdom, or Hannover in Germany—the goal was to quantify what those fees or acquisition costs were, pool a large and predictable portfolio of existing or projected policies, and, just like in the credit card business, securitize the cash flows.

In the American Skandia securitization, actually conducted as four successive deals in 1996 and 1997, American Skandia Life Assurance Corporation sold to its parent company the right to receive future fees and charges that it expected to realize on the variable portion of a designated block of deferred annuity contracts issued during certain periods (see figure 3-8 on page 70):

Transaction	Contract Issue Date	Closing Effective Date	Period
1996-1	9/1/96	12/17/96	1/1/94 - 6/30/96
1997-1	6/1/97	7/23/97	3/1/96 - 4/30/97
1997-2	12/1/97	12/30/97	5/1/95 - 12/31/96
1997-3	12/1/97	12/30/97	5/1/96 - 10/31/97

In turn, Skandia's parent, through a trust in a private placement, issued collateralized notes secured by the rights to receive these future fees and charges. Under the terms of the purchase agreements, the rights sold by Skandia provide for its parent to receive 80% (100% for transaction 1997-3) of future mortality and expense charges and contingent deferred sales charges, after reinsurance, expected to be realized over the remaining surrender charge period of the designated contracts (six to

Table 3-2 Life Deals

Insurance Company or Agent (Vehicle Name)	Amount and Rating (S&P/Moody/Fitch/Duff)	Type of Instrument	Issue Date	Maturity	Description
American Skandia Life Assurance Corporation (ASLAC Funding Trust 1996-1)	$50.22 million present value (at 7.5% discount rate) [NA/NA/NA/BBB]	M&E fee/contingent deferred sales charge securitization	Dec. 1996		Right to receive 80% of future mortality and expense charges and contingent deferred sales charges, after reinsurance, expected to be realized over the remaining surrender charge period of the designated contracts (6 to 8 years) on variable portion of designated block of deferred annuity contracts issued during the period January 1, 1994, through June 30, 1996.
American Skandia Life Assurance Corporation (ASLAC Funding Trust 1997-1)	$58.77 million present value (at 7.5% discount rate)	M&E fee/contingent deferred sales charge securitization	Jul. 1997		Same as above, for deferred annuity contracts issued during the period March 1, 1996, through April 30, 1997.
American Skandia Life Assurance Corporation (ASLAC Funding Trust 1997-2)	$77.55 million present value (at 7.5% discount rate) [NA/NA/NA/BBB]	M&E fee/contingent deferred sales charge securitization	Dec. 1997		Same as above, for deferred annuity contracts issued during the period May 1, 1995, through December 31, 1996.
American Skandia Life Assurance Corporation (ASLAC Funding Trust 1997-3)	$58.19 million present value (at 7.5% discount rate)	M&E fee/contingent deferred sales charge securitization	Dec. 1997		Right to receive 100% of future mortality and expense charges and contingent deferred sales charges, after reinsurance, expected to be realized over the remaining surrender charge period of the designated contracts (6 to 8 years) on variable portion of designated block of deferred annuity contracts issued during the period May 1, 1996, through October 31, 1997.

Table 3-2 Life Deals, *con't.*

Insurance Company or Agent (Vehicle Name)	Amount and Rating (S&P/Moody/Fitch/Duff)	Type of Instrument	Issue Date	Maturity	Description
Hannover Re (L1) (Interpolis Re)	DEM 100 million ($55.8 mm)	M&E fee/contingent deferred sales charge securitization	Jan. 1998	3-year program (12/31/01)	Financing arrangement for life/health reinsurance portfolio involving retrocession of 75% of defined reinsurance treaties to Interpolis Re, laying off up to DEM 100 million of acquisition costs in a number of different currencies.
National Provident Institution (NPI) (Mutual Securitisation Plc.)	GBP 260 million, as follows: -GBP 140 million class A1 (7.39169%/ UKT+70 bp) [A-/A3/NR/NR] -GBP 120 million class A2 (7.5873%/ UKT+140 bp) [A-/A3/NR/NR]	Life insurance acquisition cost securitization	Apr. 1998	A1: 9/30/22 A2: 9/30/12	

Sources: Goldman Sachs, SEC filings, and company press releases. While the information contained in this report was obtained from sources believed to be reliable, no guarantee can be made as to its accuracy or completeness.

Figure 3-8 American Skandia Life Assurance Corporation Flow of Funds

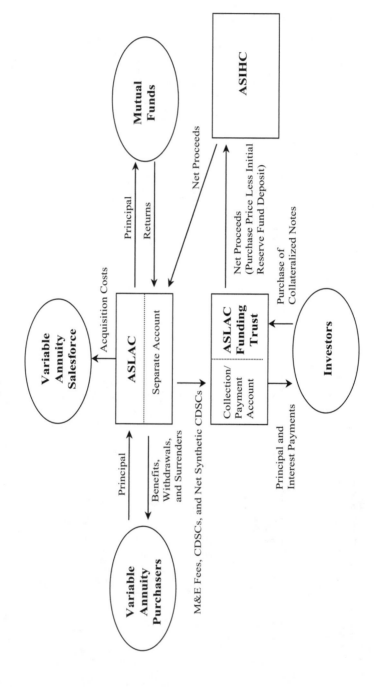

eight years). Skandia received the present value of the transactions (discounted at 7.5%) in the sale, effectively monetizing its future assets.

The UK mutual life insurer National Provident Institution (NPI) similarly securitized the future profits of a block of its insurance policies through Mutual Securitisation Plc. (see figure 3-9 on page 72). The issuance of Mutual Securitisation's GBP 260 million limited recourse bonds, due in 2012 and 2022, was the first public securitization of emerging surplus by a UK insurance company. The deal gave National Provident access to cash flows it would not otherwise have had until any surplus emerged in the future, thus providing the company with greater financial flexibility to expand its business. National Provident could have sought reinsurance financing, but that is difficult to do for a deal of this size without having additional bank resources. Securitization was also less expensive, even taking into account upfront advisor costs, because the cost of servicing capital through securitization can be far lower than for reinsurance financing. Another factor that made securitization more attractive was the time frame, as surpluses can be securitized over 20 years, whereas reinsurance would not be given beyond 10.

Finally, in another life securitization innovation, Germany's Hannover Re secured a pioneering three-year asset swap worth DEM 100 million ($55.8 million) from Rabobank to finance its aggressive drive into the European life reassurance market (see figure 3-10 on page 73). This facility, incepted January 1, 1998, allows Hannover Re to absorb life acquisition expenses from its growing presence in Germany, Austria, Italy, France, the United Kingdom, and Scandinavia. Since acquisition costs cannot be deferred under Germany's conservative accounting rules, and traditional retrocessional capacity had been exhausted, Hannover Re had to look for a new way to provide immediate balance sheet relief.

With Rabobank, Hannover Re effectively entered into a quota share arrangement similar to what conventionally exists between a reinsurer and a life company. In this case, Hannover Re shares new business with its clients in return for a share of earnings from policies in force in the years ahead. The earnings stream is passed on to a Dublin-based special purpose vehicle owned by Rabobank, Interpolis Re, in return for upfront capital. The deal, dubbed L1, allows Hannover Re to retrocede 75% of defined reinsurance treaties to Interpolis Re, laying off up to DEM 100 million of acquisition costs in a number of different currencies. The liquidity financing is provided by Rabobank and the reassurance risk is absorbed by Interpolis Re.

Figure 3-9 Mutual Securitisation Plc. Flow of Funds

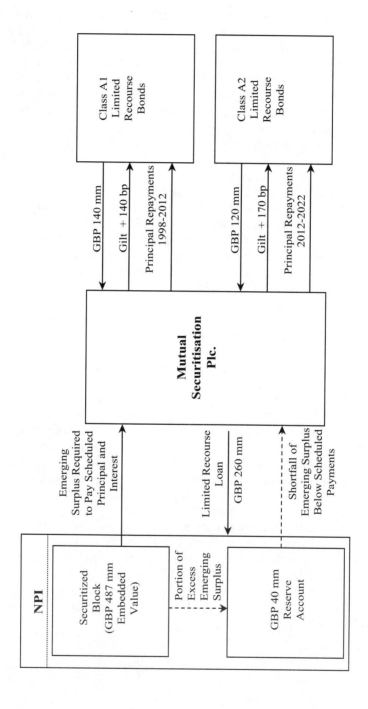

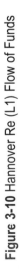

Figure 3-10 Hannover Re (L1) Flow of Funds

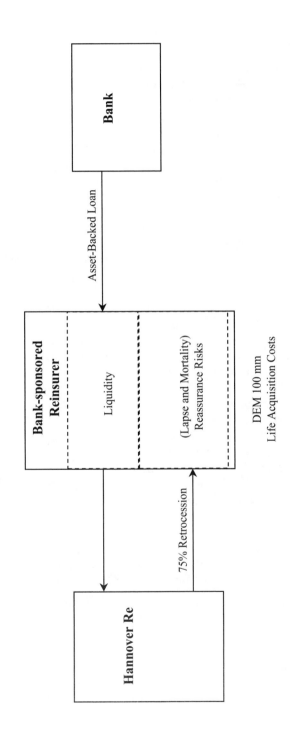

A Blurry World

The markets continue to evolve at a dramatic pace, as financial products are developed to help manage the ever-increasing number and complexity of risks managed by corporations. Second-generation products— whether structured notes, swaps, or other forms of OTC derivatives, asset- or liability-backed securities—are helping to further the types and sources of financial products that may be used for either risk-mitigation or risk-financing (capital/surplus generation) needs.

In fact, some important changes are underway in the financial services sector that may influence the pace and nature of how derivatives and securitizations will be used going forward. FASB Statement No. 133, Accounting for Derivative Instruments and Hedging Activities, was issued on June 16, 1998. Although Statement 133 is effective for fiscal years beginning after June 15, 1999, the standard may be applied early, as of the beginning of any fiscal quarter that begins after the standard's issuance date.

The FASB statement visibly shows just how much the worlds of insurance and derivatives now overlap, and how difficult it may be to separate them. To properly account for their derivative activities, corporations must now try to distinguish between insurance and derivative structures, just at a time when they are becoming more and more difficult to distinguish. For example, to the extent that a particular product or contract is not traded on an exchange, it will not be subject to FAS133, if the underlying on which settlement is based is itself based on a "climatic or geological variable or other physical variable."[1] That provides some clarification, but raises new questions of its own. To help, FASB established a Derivatives Implementation Group to clarify and assist in the implementation of FAS133. Yet witness, however straightforward FASB's clarification, how inseparable insurance and derivatives have become:

> *Question:* A contract's payment provision specifies that the issuer will pay to the holder $10,000,000 if hurricane losses for the state of Florida exceed $50,000,000 during the year 2001. Is such a contract included in the scope of Statement 133?
>
> *Response:* Yes. The underlying in this example is a financial variable (i.e., losses exceeding a specified dollar limit) rather than a climatic or physical variable (e.g., flood-water levels). Therefore, the derivative contract does not qualify for the scope exclusion in paragraph

---

[1] Financial Accounting Standards Board, Statement of Financial Accounting Standards No. 133, Accounting for Derivative Instruments and Hedging Activities, paragraph 10e, page 6.

10(e) of Statement 133. However, if the contract were to require the holder to incur a loss of revenue or an increase in expense as a condition of payoff, and the amount of the payoff was compensation for that loss, the contract would be excluded from the scope of Statement 133 because paragraph 10(e) excludes traditional insurance contracts.

In contrast, if the contract specified that the issuer pays the holder $10,000,000 in the event that there is a hurricane in Florida, the contract would qualify for the scope exclusion in paragraph 10(e) of Statement 133. In that contract, the underlying is a hurricane in Florida, which is a physical variable.[2]

As both the cases in this chapter and the above accounting announcement demonstrate, the financial world continues to blur. The increasing complexity of products will only make it harder to truly separate what is an insurance contract and what is a security or derivative structure.

---

[2] Derivatives Implementation Group, 9/1/98 Agenda Item 18, Inquiry Resolved by FASB Staff.

Legal and Regulatory Issues Affecting Insurance Derivatives and Securitization

Michael P. Goldman
Michael J. Pinsel
Natalie Spadaccini Rosenberg
Katten Muchin & Zavis

Introduction

Market observers often describe the recent emergence of insurance derivative and securitization transactions as "the convergence of the insurance and capital markets." Stated in somewhat less dramatic terms, such alternative risk-financing techniques typically involve the funding of traditional property and casualty risk through capital market transactions not traditionally applied to property and casualty risk. The underlying risk is not extraordinary (property and casualty risk has always existed), nor are the subject financial structures and instruments necessarily unique (derivative and securitization models have existed for more than a decade). Instead, it is the application of such structures and instruments to the existing risk that is truly extraordinary and unique. The legal and regulatory issues inherent in these alternative risk-financing techniques follow a similar line. While there is an existing body of law and regulation relating to insurance and reinsurance (as a traditional means for financing property and casualty risk) and existing legal and regulatory schemes relating to derivative and securitization transactions (as they have been

77

used to manage traditional financial and investment risk), the legal and regulatory issues become extraordinary and unique as these markets converge.

At a minimum, the emerging insurance derivative and securitization market has demonstrated that economic substance can take a variety of legal forms. For instance, although property and casualty risk has traditionally been financed through the procurement of insurance and reinsurance, a specified level of such risk can be funded through a variety of financial market mechanisms, including the purchase and sale of option contracts on the Chicago Board of Trade (CBOT), the issuance of insurance-linked securities, or the procurement of an over-the-counter (OTC) derivative instrument. Similarly, while the most common financial risks (e.g., interest rate, currency, market, etc.) are traditionally hedged through exchange-traded and OTC derivative strategies, such risks could be funded through the procurement of an insurance policy with appropriately structured attachment points and limits.

Most legal and regulatory models focus on a given form of transaction, accompanied by the flexibility to look to the substance of a specific transaction if circumstances dictate. Definitional examples of this premise can be found in the Securities Act of 1933's (Securities Act) definition of "security,"[1] the Commodity Exchange Act's (CEA) definition of "commodity,"[2] and the National Association of Insurance

---

[1] Section 2(1) of the Securities Act defines the term "security" in very broad terms. Not only does Section 2(1) list specific instruments, including notes, stock, and bonds, but it also contains a series of general catch-all phrases which include instruments of a more variable character. Specifically, Section 2(1) defines a "security" as "any note, stock, treasury stock, bond, debenture, evidence of indebtedness, certificate of interest or participation in any profit-sharing agreement, collateral-trust certificate, preorganization certificate or subscription, transferable share, investment contract, voting-trust certificate, certificate of deposit for a security, fractional undivided interest in oil, gas, or other mineral rights, any put, call, straddle, option, or privilege on any security, certificate of deposit, or group or index of securities (including any interest therein or based on the value thereof), or any put, call, straddle, option, or privilege entered into on a national securities exchange relating to foreign currency, or, in general, any interest or instrument commonly known as a 'security,' or any certificate of interest or participation in, temporary or interim certificate for, receipt for, guarantee of, or warrant or right to subscribe to or purchase, any of the foregoing."

[2] Section 1a(3) of the CEA defines the term "commodity" as "all . . . goods and articles . . . and all services, rights and interests in which contracts for future delivery are presently or in the future dealt in." Like the Securities Act definition of a "security," this is a broad, catch-all definition designed to encompass all types of commodity products.

Commissioners (NAIC)[3] Investments of Insurers Model Act's (Defined Limits Version) (NAIC Model Investment Law) definition of "derivative instrument."[4] In each instance, the statutory definition consists of a list of specific instruments, as well as a conceptual or general definition to address those items appropriately covered by the subject regulatory scheme but not necessarily among the enumerated terms. Because insurance derivative and securitization transactions involve the funding of traditional risk in a form not traditionally applied to such risk, more than one regulatory scheme may apply to a given transaction. As such, to address the legal and regulatory issues inherent in such transactions, it is essential to look to both the form and substance of the transaction and then to identify the applicable regulatory scheme(s).

This chapter will categorize various forms of insurance derivative and securitization transactions that have occurred to date in order to identify the various legal and regulatory schemes that will govern or otherwise affect such transactions. In addition, we will provide a brief overview of those regulatory systems which invariably will apply to the generic categories of insurance derivative and securitization transactions, as well as identify certain legal and regulatory issues underlying specific structural forms. Finally, because a large majority of insurance derivative and securitization transactions are designed to finance risks germane to insurance companies, we will address the current regulatory authority of U.S.-based insurance and reinsurance companies to engage in such transactions for both hedging and speculative purposes. While this chapter will identify and discuss a variety of legal and regulatory issues, it will not necessarily resolve these issues, due to the extraordinarily fact-specific nature of most insurance derivative and securitization transactions.

---

[3] The NAIC is a quasi-regulatory association, composed of the chief insurance regulator from each U.S. jurisdiction, which is intended to promote uniformity among state regulatory systems. In addition to promulgating model laws and regulations, which have force and effect only if specifically adopted by individual state legislatures, the NAIC also establishes the financial reporting forms and accounting and valuation practices and procedures to which all states defer in their respective insurance regulatory systems.

[4] The NAIC Model Investment Law defines a "derivative instrument" as an "agreement, option, instrument or a series or combination thereof to make or take delivery of, or assume or relinquish, a specified amount of one or more underlying interests, or to make a cash settlement in lieu thereof; or that has a price, performance, value or cash flow based primarily upon the actual or expected price, level, performance, value or cash flow of one or more underlying interests." In addition to giving this specific definition of a "derivative instrument," the NAIC Model Investment Law also lists a series of instruments included under the definition. These instruments include "options, warrants used in a hedging transaction and not attached to another financial instrument, caps, floors, collars, swaps, forwards, futures and any other agreements, options or instruments substantially similar thereto or any series or combination thereof and any agreements, options or instruments permitted under regulations" implementing the NAIC Model Investment Law.

Definitions and Transaction Structures

Included within the traditional and emerging risk-financing markets are a variety of transaction structures, and the terms used to describe these structures have become so commonplace that they are often subject to misunderstanding and incorrect application. Because structural form and categorization are important to the identification and application of the regulatory scheme(s) that will govern a given alternative risk-financing mechanism, a brief summary of the types of transactions that have been undertaken to date and the placement of such transactions into categories of legal and regulatory significance is a logical first step to a more complete analysis.

Although there is a seemingly wide variety of possible alternative risk-financing structures, all such transactions can be placed into one of four broad categories: insurance/reinsurance, insurance derivatives, insurance securitization, and liquidity and contingent capital facilities.

Insurance/Reinsurance. In the most generic context, "insurance" may be defined as the transfer of risk from one party who is directly subject to such risk (the insured) to another party who is in the business of assuming such risk (the insurer) by means of an insurance contract or policy. "Reinsurance" may be similarly defined as the transfer of risk from a party who has already assumed such risk from another (the ceding insurer) to another party who is in the business of assuming such risk (the reinsurer) by means of a reinsurance contract or treaty.[5] Insurance/reinsurance can transfer all components of an underlying risk (i.e., underwriting and timing), or it can principally address timing risk, with less-than-complete transfer of subject underwriting risk. The latter form of coverage is often referred to as "finite risk" or financial insurance/reinsurance and may be treated as a financing mechanism under applicable accounting or reporting models.

---

[5] The foregoing definitions are admittedly incomplete (and of limited practical use) because they are dependent on the risk-transfer mechanism's being an insurance or reinsurance contract or the assuming party, being an insurer or reinsurer. Although labeling the risk-transfer mechanism an "insurance/reinsurance contract" and having the assuming party be an insurance or reinsurance company can invoke applicable insurance regulation, the lack of such label and existing regulatory status will not necessarily exempt a given transaction from insurance regulation. See section titled "The Insurance Regulatory System and Corresponding Legal and Regulatory Issues."

Insurance derivatives. "Insurance derivatives" involve the transfer of property and casualty risk through the issuance of one or more "derivative instruments."[6] "Insurance commoditization," which is a subset of the more general insurance derivatives category, involves a standardized index or other reference base and a corresponding futures and/or option contract traded on a commodity futures exchange. Examples of insurance derivatives include risk commoditization products like the CBOT's complex of catastrophe options or similar products traded on the newly formed Bermuda Commodities Exchange, as well as OTC products like loss ratio caps and risk-referenced total return swaps.

Insurance securitization. "Insurance securitization" involves the transfer of property and casualty risk from one party who has assumed (or is otherwise subject to) property and casualty risk (the issuer) to another party (the investor) pursuant to the issuance of a security (e.g., debt or preferred stock), the ultimate return on which is dependent on the occurrence or nonoccurrence of one or more referenced events, the performance of a referenced index, or the experience of an actual or hypothetical portfolio of insurance business. The security can either be subject to principal invasion or be "principal-protected," with variable coupon and/or extension of maturity providing the underlying risk funding. The issuer is typically a special purpose reinsurer (SPR), which underwrites an insurance/reinsurance contract for the subject entity (insured, insurer, or reinsurer) and then issues insurance-linked securities to fund its exposure under such insurance/reinsurance contract. Examples include recent offerings by Residential Reinsurance Limited (United Services Automobile Association and USAA Casualty Insurance Company), George Town Re, Ltd. (St. Paul Reinsurance Company Limited), SLF Reinsurance, Ltd. (Reliance National), SR Earthquake Fund, Ltd. (Swiss Reinsurance Company) Parametric Re (Tokio Marine & Fire Insurance Company, Ltd.), Trinity Re (Centre Solutions Ltd.), Pacific Re Ltd. (Yasuda Fire & Marine Insurance Company), and Mosaic Re (F&G Re).

Liquidity and Contingent Capital Facilities. "Liquidity and contingent capital facilities" do not necessarily involve the transfer of risk. Instead, such strategies typically involve a prenegotiated obligation to provide financial support to a given insured, insurer, or reinsurer upon the occurrence of a specified trigger, or without regard to any

---

[6] See footnote 4.

trigger, upon the election of the covered party. Liquidity facilities are often designed to provide funds for the payment of losses during the initial periods following a catastrophic or other event; the funds must be repaid (with interest) over a specified term. Such liquidity facilities have been placed with a syndicate of financial institutions for the Florida Windstorm Fund and several large commercial insurance companies. Contingent capital facilities provide the subject entity with the right to "put" its equity to the contingent investor. The specific attributes of such equity (e.g., common versus preferred, convertibility, dividend rights, etc.) vary from transaction to transaction. Examples include the catastrophe equity puts that Aon Group arranged for RLI Corp. and Horace Mann Educators Corporation, as well as the contingent surplus note facilities in place with Nationwide Mutual Insurance Company, Arkwright Mutual Insurance Company, and LaSalle Re Holdings, Ltd.

Most of the foregoing transaction structures are designed to transfer property and casualty risk from one party to another. In contrast, finite risk reinsurance and liquidity and contingent capital facilities are often considered financing arrangements, because there is an obligation to repay the funds provided (in the case of finite risk reinsurance and liquidity facilities) or a lack of any specific risk-related trigger (in the case of many contingent capital facilities). Because true risk-transfer structures present some of the more intriguing legal and regulatory issues underlying the emerging alternative risk-financing market, we will focus on those transactions which irrevocably and permanently transfer property and casualty risk from one party to another, specifically, insurance/reinsurance, insurance derivatives, and insurance securitization.

The Insurance Regulatory System and Corresponding Legal and Regulatory Issues

Regulation of Insurance and Reinsurance in the United States

To understand the legal and regulatory issues inherent in the developing alternative property and casualty risk-transfer marketplace, it is necessary to have some appreciation for the regulatory system that traditionally has applied to property and casualty risk transfer. Such an appreciation is important because the insurance regulatory system will clearly govern certain components of insurance securitization transactions (e.g., the formation and operation of the SPR and the reinsurance transaction between the ceding insurer and the SPR, including any reinsurance security arrangement), as well as the use of insurance companies as "transformers" in certain insurance derivative transactions. Additionally, participants in insurance derivative and securitization transactions, including underwriters, broker/dealers, and investors, could possibly be considered to be "conducting an insurance business," potentially invoking certain insurance laws and regulations.

The "Business of Insurance"

In the United States,[7] insurance is regulated on a state-by-state basis, and the supremacy of state law over federal law with respect to the "business of insurance" is generally confirmed by the McCarran-Ferguson Act.[8] A central issue with respect to the regulation of insurance is what constitutes the "business of insurance." The United States Supreme Court has examined this issue in various contexts[9] to determine if a particular business is subject to federal law or if such federal law is preempted by state law governing such business as the "business of insurance."

In 1979, the U.S. Supreme Court granted *certiorari* in *Group Life and Health Ins. Co. v. Royal Drug Co.*[10] to resolve intercircuit conflicts regarding the meaning of the phrase "business of insurance." As articulated in a later U.S. Supreme Court opinion, the Court in *Group Life* essentially identified:

> three criteria relevant in determining whether a particular practice is part of the "business of insurance". . .: first, whether the practice has the effect of transferring or spreading a policyholder's risk; second, whether the practice is an integral part of the

---

[7] While insurance and reinsurance companies, intermediaries, and risks increasingly cross global boundaries, a discussion of insurance and other regulation outside the United States is beyond the scope of this chapter.

[8] The McCarran-Ferguson Act, 15 U.S.C. §1012(a), provides that "the business of insurance, and every person engaged therein, shall be subject to the laws of the several States which relate to the regulation or taxation of such business." The Act also provides that "no Act of Congress shall be construed to invalidate, impair, or supersede any law enacted by any State for the purpose of regulating the business of insurance . . . unless such Act specifically relates to the business of insurance."

[9] The issue of what constitutes the "business of insurance" has been examined by the U.S. Supreme Court in the context of determining whether a business is subject to the Sherman Act antitrust laws and also in the context of preemption under the Employee Retirement Income Security Act of 1974. See, e.g., *Group Life & Health Ins. Co. v. Royal Drug Co.*, 440 U.S. 205 (1979); *Union Labor Life Ins. Co. v. Pireno*, 458 U.S. 119 (1982); *Metro. Life Ins. Co. v. MA Travelers Ins. Co.*, 471 U.S. 724 (1985); and *Pilot Life Ins. Co. v. Dedeaux*, 481 U.S. 41 (1987).

[10] *Group Life*, 440 U.S. 205.

policy relationship between the insurer and the insured; and third, whether the practice is limited to entities within the insurance industry.[11]

In determining whether a practice constitutes the "business of insurance," these three criteria must be examined as a whole because, as the Court indicated, "none of these criteria are necessarily determinative in itself."

Although the U.S. Supreme Court has advanced these criteria in determining whether a practice constitutes the "business of insurance," according to the McCarran-Ferguson Act, each state has the authority to statutorily define the term and, where a state has not statutorily defined the term, state courts have the authority to assert their own interpretations. While most states examine some of the same criteria as those recognized in *Group Life*, a discussion of the nuances of the criteria used in different states is beyond the scope of this chapter.

Regulation of Insurers, Reinsurers, and Intermediaries

For the most part, the financial condition of an insurance company is regulated by the state in which it is domiciled.[12] The business of insurance generally is regulated to protect consumers. Consequently, regulation focuses primarily on the products and the methods by which such products are offered to the insured, as well as on the financial strength and solvency of the insurance company, to ensure that it will be able to fulfill its contractual obligations to the underlying policyholders. Consumer-protection-oriented regulation, for example, mandates certain policy provisions and disclosures, provides for certain procedures to cancel policies, and requires the licensure of insurance and reinsurance agents, brokers, and intermediaries. Financial-oriented regulation includes requiring licensure to offer lines of insurance business, mandating minimum capital and surplus (net worth) levels, specifying qualitative and quantitative investment parameters, setting forth underwriting limitations, and providing for limitations, disclosures, and approval requirements relating to transactions with affiliates, the payment of dividends to stockholders, and changes in company control. While the financial condition of an insurance company generally is regulated by the state in which it is domiciled,

---

[11] *Union Labor Life Ins. Co.*, 458 U.S. at 129.

[12] The insurance codes of certain states (e.g., New York) take an "extraterritorial" regulatory approach to insurance companies that are merely licensed in the state.

the laws of the state in which the insured or the covered risk is located generally will govern the form of the insurance product and the method by which the insurance product is distributed, as well as the licensure or qualification of the entity to engage in such activities.

Whereas the regulatory scheme relating to the sale of primary insurance generally focuses on the party that will bear the risk (the insurer), the regulation of reinsurance generally focuses on the party receiving coverage (the ceding insurer) by limiting the financial statement "credit" the ceding insurer can receive in connection with a reinsurance arrangement unless the reinsurer meets certain statutory requirements. Such statutory "credit for reinsurance" typically will be allowed only if (i) the reinsurer is licensed to transact insurance in the state of domicile of the ceding insurer; (ii) the reinsurer is "accredited" in the ceding insurer's state of domicile, a status achieved by making certain filings with the ceding insurer's state of domicile and meeting certain financial requirements; or (iii) certain security is provided by the reinsurer (e.g., funds retained by the ceding insurer, funds held in trust, or letters of credit), subject to specific statutory requirements.

In addition to the insurance codes and regulations of each state, insurance companies are also affected by specific guidance developed by the NAIC. While the model laws and regulations promulgated by the NAIC have no force or effect unless specifically adopted by individual state legislatures or departments of insurance, the NAIC does establish the financial reporting forms and accounting and valuation practices and procedures to which all states defer in their respective insurance regulatory systems. For example, the NAIC, through its committee structure, establishes the financial reporting by insurance companies of insurance derivatives and the "buy-side" of insurance securitizations. Similarly, the Securities Valuation Office of the NAIC (SVO)[13] reviews, rates, and values certain securities in accordance with NAIC guidance, and the SVO-established treatment of such securities (such as whether they will be considered debt or equity) will impact the financial reporting and risk-based capital[14] implications of certain securities.

---

[13] The SVO, a division of the NAIC, is intended to promote uniformity in the statutory reporting of insurers' investments by providing an independent source of investment information to state insurance regulatory officials.

[14] Risk-based capital is a financial adequacy measurement method, established by the NAIC, intended to identify the minimum required level of capitalization of an insurer, taking into account the underwriting, credit, investment, and other business risks inherent in the insurer's operations.

Separate from and in addition to the regulation of the risk-bearing entity, insurance and reinsurance intermediaries (i.e., agents and brokers) generally are required to be licensed in, and are regulated by, the states in which they operate. To be licensed as an insurance or reinsurance intermediary, an individual applicant generally must submit an application and pass an examination that demonstrates that the applicant is competent and trustworthy. Such intermediaries are subject to certain disclosure requirements relating to their sales of insurance products to insureds and reinsureds, as well as to certain financial responsibilities, such as the maintenance of customer funds in a specialized premium fund trust account.

To see how existing insurance regulation can apply to an emerging market, consider the New York-based Catastrophe Risk Exchange (CATEX), established in 1996 to facilitate the exchange of property and casualty insurance risks based upon market-established relative pricing. CATEX essentially acts as an intermediary between insurance companies with respect to the transfer of portfolios of insurance business. In this regard, CATEX was required by New York insurance regulators to be licensed as a reinsurance intermediary. Interestingly, while CATEX (which was established for the sole purpose of serving as a market on which to trade insurance risks) was required to be licensed as a reinsurance intermediary, the CBOT (which traditionally has served as a market on which to trade agricultural and financial risks in the form of futures and option contracts and only recently began to serve as a market for trading insurance-related risks) has not been required to be licensed as a reinsurance intermediary. This disparity in regulatory treatment likely is due to the form of the underlying instrument of risk transfer (i.e., a reinsurance contract as opposed to an index-based option). Although not determinative, the fact that the CBOT is already subject to the primary regulation of the Commodity Futures Trading Commission (CFTC) may have reduced the level of insurance regulatory scrutiny to which it otherwise may have been subject.[15]

Use of Insurance/Reinsurance to Fund Traditional and Nontraditional Risks

Historically, insurance and reinsurance have been used to fund traditional property and casualty risks, such as physical damage to property and the imposition of legal liability. While the traditional notions of "insurance" relate to monetary protection from property damage or the

---

[15] See section titled "Futures Regulation."

imposition of legal liability, the insurance industry has recently begun to assume a role in the transfer of more general and varied types of risks, applying its risk-assessment expertise and financial resources to nontraditional areas. For example, while the risks of fluctuations in interest rates, currency rates, and portfolio values are traditionally managed through OTC and exchange-traded derivative transactions, certain insurance organizations have expressed a willingness to consider the expansion of their traditional products to address certain financial risks. In this regard, "package" insurance policies are emerging that combine coverage for traditional property and casualty insurance risks with coverages to address financial risks, such as currency risks. Honeywell Inc., for example, recently purchased a multiyear insurance policy covering property, liability, workers' compensation, and currency exposures.[16]

Insurance companies also have begun to offer customized policies to cover risks outside the traditional property and casualty insurance realm. These unique programs include insurance of financial risks, regarding subjects such as tax-benefit qualification and recapture, mergers, acquisitions, and corporate restructurings (including representations and warranties contained in documentation relating thereto),[17] and protection of nonqualified executive compensation benefits. To the extent that insurance companies offer forms of insurance to cover financial and investment risks, such as policies to protect against fluctuations in interest rates (as an alternative to interest rate caps, floors, and collars), policies to protect against decreases in the value of investment portfolios (as an alternative to certain options, forwards, and futures), and others, it follows that regulatory schemes beyond those applicable to the business of insurance may affect the underlying transaction. For example, if an insurance policy includes an embedded option or references a commodity index, the insurance company may be unexpectedly subject to certain aspects of securities or commodity futures regulation. Similarly, insurance and reinsurance intermediaries could be subject to corresponding Securities and Exchange Commission (SEC) or CFTC oversight, based on their specific roles in the issuance of such a policy.

---

[16] Carolyn T. Gear, "Who Needs Derivatives?" (Insurance), *Forbes,* April 21, 1997, page 52. The authors understand that at the time this article was published in *Forbes,* the subject policy had not yet been issued; subsequently, such package policy became effective.

[17] Such programs are underwritten by the London-based Tax and Financial Risks Indemnity Line Slip, for example.

Implications of Insurance Regulation on Insurance Derivatives and Securitization

Just as the coverage of certain financial market risks within an insurance policy may invoke other regulatory schemes, the financing of traditional property and casualty risk through "alternative" capital market transaction forms, such as insurance derivatives or securitization, may invoke certain insurance regulation. Such issues usually arise in the context of whether the assuming party will be considered to be "conducting an insurance business," thereby subjecting it to the insurance regulatory schemes described above. In this regard, the purchasers, holders, owners, or writers of insurance derivative or securitization products could be required to be licensed, authorized, or qualified as insurers or reinsurers. Similarly, the underwriters, selling agents, and broker/dealers of insurance derivative and securitization products could be required to be licensed as insurance or reinsurance agents, brokers, or intermediaries in all relevant jurisdictions.

As is often the case, the marketplace may develop more rapidly than the regulations governing the marketplace. In this regard, the regulatory schemes that govern noninsurance industry entities that wish to broker or bear traditional insurance risks in nontraditional forms are not well established or well documented. Consequently, noninsurance industry entities should consider whether they are unwittingly subjecting themselves to existing insurance regulation when they assume risk through, or act as an intermediary with respect to, insurance derivative and securitization products. The question of whether an entity is "conducting an insurance business" will arise in the context of most alternative risk-financing transactions.

Insurance Derivatives

The universe of insurance derivatives can be divided into two major categories: exchange-traded (commoditized) insurance derivatives and OTC insurance derivatives. The exchange-traded products include the CBOT's complex of standardized catastrophe options, which are based on Property Claim Services (PCS) catastrophe loss indices, as well as the complex of options traded on the newly formed Bermuda Commodities Exchange. Such contracts are promoted as a risk-transfer mechanism which allows insurers and reinsurers to supplement traditional reinsurance programs, hedge retention levels, and geographically diversify risk exposure. The parties to each trade bear financial risk relating to the changes or lack of changes in the underlying indices, which are based on certain insured property losses.

OTC insurance derivatives include a broad spectrum of instruments and transactions which can be customized to fit the specific needs of each particular party and situation. One example of an OTC insurance derivative is a loss ratio cap, in which a party agrees to provide payments to an insurer in the event that such insurer's loss ratio exceeds a set limit within a set time period. In such a transaction, the insurer pays the cap writer a premium at the inception of the trade, and the cap writer bears some or all of the risk that the insurer may exceed the set loss ratio limit. Another example of a OTC insurance derivative is a total return swap that involves a referenced insurance-linked security. Such a swap involves the holder of an insurance-linked security offering to pay another party an amount equal to the total investment return on the insurance-linked security in exchange for a payment from the other party that might be based upon a fixed or variable interest rate.

In all such insurance derivative transactions, property and casualty insurance risk is passed from the bearer of such risk (i.e., the insurance company or the insurance-linked security holder) to another party through one or more derivative instruments. Such instruments and transactions are subject to the traditional regulatory schemes that apply to derivatives and could be subject to certain insurance regulatory schemes.

Futures Regulation

Depending on the underlying form and economic substance of a particular insurance derivative transaction, participants could become subject to the regulatory purview of the CFTC. The CEA provides for the exclusive jurisdiction of the CFTC over contracts for future delivery of a "commodity,"[18] as well as options on a commodity (collectively, "futures contracts")[19] The CEA requires that all transactions involving a "contract for the purchase or sale of a commodity for future delivery" be effected on a designated commodities exchange[20] and generally prohibits the off-exchange trading of commodity options.[21] Notably, neither the CEA nor

---

[18] See footnote 2 for the CEA's broad definition of the term "commodity."

[19] Section 2(a)(1)(A)(i) of the CEA.

[20] Section 4(a) of the CEA.

[21] Section 4c(b) of the CEA.

the CFTC's regulations define the term "futures contract."[22] Because certain OTC derivatives can serve similar economic functions as, and share certain characteristics with, exchange-traded futures contracts, certain OTC derivatives face the possibility of falling within the judicially crafted definition of a futures contract. Similarly, because certain OTC insurance derivatives have economics and characteristics (including reference to PCS information as an index) similar to those of exchange-traded insurance derivatives (such as the catastrophe options traded on the CBOT, which are clearly subject to CFTC jurisdiction), such OTC insurance derivatives face futures-related (as well as insurance-related) legal and regulatory uncertainty. Instruments, including all CBOT insurance options and any OTC insurance derivatives, determined to be "futures contracts" will be subject to CFTC regulation and the CEA's exchange-trading requirement. There are, however, several narrow exemptions from regulation under the CEA and to the exchange-trading requirement that may apply to OTC insurance derivatives, depending upon the form and economic substance of such products.[23]

---

[22] The CFTC and the courts have identified certain elements as necessary, but not always sufficient, for defining a contract as a futures contract. These elements are: (1) the obligation of each party at the inception of the contract to fulfill the contract at a specified price; (2) the use of the contract to shift or assume the risk of price changes; and (3) the ability to satisfy the contract by either making or accepting delivery of the underlying commodity or offsetting the original contract with another contract. The CFTC and the courts have also identified additional elements that characterize exchange-traded futures contracts, including standardized terms (e.g., the type, grade, and amount of the underlying commodity), the posting of performance bonds (i.e., margin) by both parties, the use of a clearinghouse that mutualizes the risk of counterparty default, open and competitive trading, and price dissemination. Although these additional elements characterize (and facilitate) trading of futures contracts on exchanges, they do not necessarily define what makes a contract a futures contract. The requirement that a futures contract be traded on an exchange is what makes the contract legal under the CEA, but is not what makes a contract a futures contract. Because the CFTC and the courts have characterized futures contracts in a way that reflects their economic risk-shifting function, the term "futures contract" potentially covers other risk-shifting products that are not typically exchange-traded.

[23] See, for example, the CEA's exemption for cash forward contracts (Section 1a(11) of the CEA); the CFTC's Statutory Interpretation Concerning Forward Transactions (September 25, 1990); the so-called "Treasury Amendment" relating to transactions in foreign currency and other instruments such as security warrants, security rights, resales of installment loan contracts, repurchase options, government securities, or mortgage and mortgage purchase commitments not traded on an exchange (Section 2(a)(1)(A) of the CEA); a limited exemption from the exchange-trading requirement for "trade options" (CFTC Regulation 32.4(a)); the "Shad-Johnson Accord" regarding SEC jurisdiction over options on securities (see footnote 29 below); the CFTC's July 1989 Swaps Policy Statement; the CFTC's Part 35 Swaps Exemption under the Futures Trading Practices Act of 1992; the CFTC's Part 34 Hybrids Exemption; the CFTC's Exemption for Certain Contracts Involving Energy Products; and the CFTC's exemptive authority under Section 4(c)(1) of the CEA, which permits the CFTC to exempt any agreement, contract, or transaction that is otherwise subject to the exchange-trading requirement from any provision of the CEA (except for the Shad-Johnson Accord) if the CFTC determines that such exemption would be consistent with the public interest.

If a particular insurance derivative product is deemed to be a futures contract, absent an applicable exemption, transactions in the product, as well as parties and intermediaries to the transaction, will be subject to the jurisdiction, regulation, and exchange-trading[24] requirement of the CEA and the CFTC. The CFTC implements regulations with which exchanges, industry professionals, and parties to futures contracts must comply. For example, CFTC regulations require futures market intermediaries to, among other things, register with the CFTC,[25] provide risk disclosures to futures contract customers, segregate customer funds, comply with recordkeeping and customer order audit trail requirements, and meet regulatory capital and other financial requirements. Futures contract customers are subject to speculative position limits, large-trader reporting requirements, performance bond requirements, and CFTC regulations

---

[24] The economic function of the futures exchanges is to provide a mechanism for price discovery and a means for offsetting price risk. Futures exchanges (through their clearinghouses) also provide a trade settlement and clearance function. Settlement is the process of fulfilling contractual requirements through cash payment or delivery of the commodity. Clearance is the process of collecting trade data, reconciling the buyers' and sellers' submission of trade data, and guaranteeing the settlement of the trade once the trade data is matched. In addition, futures exchanges serve a self-regulatory function. Futures exchanges must be approved by, and operate under the oversight of, the CFTC. Futures exchanges list standardized contracts, adopt and enforce rules regarding trading of contracts and the conduct of exchange members, set qualification standards for membership on the exchange, monitor trading activity for manipulation and other illegal conduct, examine member compliance with financial requirements, respond to customer inquiries, and provide a venue for resolution of customer complaints.

[25] With certain limited exceptions, all individuals and organizations that intend to do business as futures professionals are required to be registered with the CFTC and to become members of the National Futures Association. The categories of industry professionals subject to the CFTC's registration requirement include: Futures Commission Merchants (FCMs), which are entities that both solicit or accept orders to buy or sell futures contracts and accept money from customers to support such orders (equivalent to a broker/dealer in the securities industry); Introducing Brokers (IBs), which are entities that solicit or accept orders to buy or sell futures contracts, but do not handle customer funds; Commodity Trading Advisors (CTAs), which are entities that engage in the business of advising others with respect to transactions in futures (equivalent to an investment advisor in the securities industry); Commodity Pool Operators (CPOs), which are entities that operate or solicit funds for collective investment vehicles (such as commodity pools or funds); Associated Persons (APs), who are individuals who solicit orders, customers, or funds on behalf of an FCM, IB, CTA, or CPO (the equivalent of a registered representative under securities regulation); Floor Brokers (FBs), who are individuals that purchase or sell futures contracts on the floor of an exchange for the FB's personal account and any other person; and Floor Traders (FTs), who are individuals that trade futures contracts on the floor of an exchange only for their personal accounts. Applicants for registration are subject to a fitness inquiry, which includes an examination requirement, background check, and a fingerprinting requirement. Additionally, all 10% or more beneficial owners or contributors of capital, and officers and directors of an FCM, IB, CTA, or CPO are required to be identified to the CFTC and are subject to a background and fingerprint check.

that proscribe noncompetitive, manipulative, or fraudulent trading practices (such as wash sales and prearranged trades). The futures industry functions under a scheme of self-regulation and federal oversight in much the same way as the securities industry.[26] The CFTC maintains its oversight function by requiring approval of new and amended exchange rules, conducting surveillance of the markets, and inspecting the exchanges to determine how well they regulate themselves. Direct regulation by the CFTC is effected through its independent investigations into illegal activities and prosecution of alleged violators of the CEA and CFTC regulations.

Securities Regulation

Writers and dealers of OTC derivatives also must be aware of the potential applicability and implications of federal and state securities laws.[27] Section 2(1) of the Securities Act defines the term "security" very broadly to include certain derivatives, such as (i) options on securities or groups or indices of securities and (ii) options entered into on a national securities exchange relating to any interest or instrument commonly known as a "security."[28] In the event that the derivative instrument at issue is found to be a "security" under the provisions of the Securities Act, such security must be registered with the SEC and applicable state agencies in connection with its offering, unless an applicable exemption from registration is available. Although many OTC derivative trades are "one-off" transactions which commonly are not considered to be the types of transactions that invoke the registration requirements of the Securities Act, the antifraud provisions of the Securities Act nevertheless apply to the offering and sale of an OTC insurance derivative that is a "security"[29] under this regulatory scheme.

---

[26] See section titled "Securities Regulation" under "Insurance Securitization."

[27] See section titled "Securities Regulation" under "Insurance Securitization."

[28] See footnote 1 above.

[29] Section 2(a)(1)(B) of the CEA and Section 9(g) of the Securities Exchange Act of 1934 (collectively, the "Shad-Johnson Accord") allocates jurisdiction between the CFTC and SEC with respect to futures, securities, and options. The CFTC has exclusive jurisdiction over futures contracts with respect to groups or indices of securities and options on such futures contracts. (Futures contracts with respect to a single security are prohibited.) The SEC has exclusive jurisdiction over securities and options on securities (or options on a securities index). However, if a product creates both a "security" and a "contract for future delivery," the CFTC has exclusive jurisdiction. (See *CME vs. SEC*, 883 F.2d 537, at 544 (7th Cir., 1989.)

Insurance derivatives structured as swaps, for example, though often not thought of as securities, still may be subject to certain aspects of federal securities regulation. Those dealing in swaps have traditionally taken the position that swaps are not securities and, as such, are not subject to federal securities regulation by the SEC. In December 1994, however, this position was called into question when the SEC issued an order stating that certain treasury-linked swaps sold by BT Securities Corporation to Gibson Greetings were securities.[30] In May 1996, the issue was examined once again when the United States District Court for the Southern District of Ohio held that two separate interest rate swap transactions between Bankers Trust and Proctor & Gamble Co. (P&G) did not constitute securities.[31]

---

[30] In the Matter of BT Securities Corp., Release Nos. 33-7124, 34-35136 (Dec. 22, 1994). In the Matter of BT Securities Corporation (BT Securities), the SEC entered into a settlement with BT Securities, an affiliate of Bankers Trust Company (Bankers Trust), which it had determined to be in violation of the reporting and antifraud provisions of the federal securities laws in connection with derivative sold by BT Securities to Gibson Greetings Inc. (Gibson). Central to the SEC's ability to find BT Securities in violation of the federal securities laws was a determination that the derivative transactions engaged in were securities as defined in Section 2(1) of the Securities Act. Of the 29 derivative transactions entered into by BT Securities and Gibson, at least one, the treasury-linked swap, was structured as a "swap." However, the SEC determined that the treasury-linked swap was a security.

With close to no explanation, the SEC stated in a footnote to the Release that "the treasury-linked swap was actually a cash-settled put option written by Gibson" based initially on the spread between the price of a U.S. Treasury security maturing on a specific date and the arithmetic average of the bid and offered yields of the most recently auctioned obligation of a two-year U.S. Treasury note. Thus, the SEC determined that the transaction consisted of an option rather than a swap and consequently was included in the definition of a "security" under the Securities Act.

The SEC repeated the determination made in the BT Securities Order in two 1996 settlement orders arising from proceedings, relating to the same transactions, against two registered representatives at BT Securities—Mitchell A. Vazquez and Gary S. Missner. (See In the Matter of Mitchell A. Vazquez, Release Nos. 33-7269, 34-36906 (Feb. 29, 1996), and In the Matter of Gary S. Missner, Release Nos. 33-7304, 34-37301 (June 11, 1996).)

[31] *Proctor & Gamble Co. v. Bankers Trust Co. and BT Securities Corp.*, 925 F. Supp. 1270 (S.D. Ohio 1996). In this case, P&G sued Bankers Trust and BT Securities for damages relating to two separate interest rate swap agreements, alleging, among other things, fraud, misrepresentation, and negligence in connection with the transactions. In analyzing whether the subject swaps were securities within the meaning of federal and state securities laws, the presiding judge examined P&G's claims that these swaps were either investment contracts, notes, evidences of indebtedness, options on securities, or instruments commonly known as securities, as outlined in the definition of a "security" in Section 2(1) of the Securities Act. In conducting his analysis, the judge examined U.S. Supreme Court precedent defining these terms (*SEC v. Howey*, 328 U.S. 293 (1946) and *Reves v. Ernst & Young*, 494 U.S. 56 (1989)) and concluded that neither swap met the definition of a "security." The judge's opinion outlined the reasons for his conclusion that the transactions were not options and noted that in the orders issued in the Gibson Greetings case, the SEC "acknowledged that its findings were solely for the purpose of effectuating the respondents' Offers of Settlement" and they were "not binding on any other person or entity named as a defendant or respondent in any other proceeding."

The issue of whether a swap is a security is far from resolved. While the SEC's orders relating to the Gibson Greetings transactions indicate the type of swap that the SEC may find to be security, these orders have little, if any, precedential value. In addition, in the P&G case, the judge emphasized that the "holdings in the [P&G] case are narrow" and stated that he did "not determine that all leveraged derivatives transactions are not securities, or that all swaps are not securities."[32] The judge further stated that "some of these derivative instruments, because of their structure, may be securities."[33] Moreover, the P&G case was heard in a district court and consequently has limited precedential value. Until the SEC or the federal courts examine this issue fully, it is impossible to say if and what types of swaps (including those based on an underlying insurance-linked product) will be considered "securities."

A determination that an OTC insurance derivative is a security could have significant implications on the marketing and distribution of such products. For example, while it is unlikely that an insurance-based swap transaction would be considered a public issuance of securities subject to the registration requirements of the Securities Act, those facilitating such swap transactions might be considered to be broker/dealers subject to regulation under the Securities Exchange Act of 1934 (the Securities Exchange Act). In light of these issues, the potential status of an OTC insurance derivative instrument as a "security" under federal and state securities laws, as well as the applicability of any offering exemption and the scope of disclosure, should be analyzed in connection with the writing and distribution of such a product to end users.[34]

Insurance Regulation

Although a writer or broker of OTC derivatives typically would not consider itself to be subject to insurance regulation, when the risk transferred is one that traditionally is the subject of insurance, insurance regulators may consider those involved in the risk transfer to be "conducting an insurance business." Although not determinative, this potential for insurance regulation is heightened if there is no other regulatory scheme that is readily applicable, such as may be the case with OTC derivatives in general and swaps in particular. For example, a hedge fund formed to

---

[32] *Id.* at 1283.
[33] *Id.*
[34] See section titled "Securities Regulation" under "Insurance Securitization."

speculate in the insurance derivatives market that writes an OTC instrument structured as a swap likely would consider such a transaction to be free from securities and futures regulation. Notwithstanding the form of the transaction, however, insurance regulators possibly could consider the transaction to be the issuance of an insurance policy and the hedge fund to be "conducting an insurance business." Under such a determination, the hedge fund could be considered to be an unauthorized insurer, thereby subject to a cease-and-desist order and other penalties. Similarly, intermediaries involved in the transaction could be considered to be producing insurance business or offering advice regarding an insurance policy without a license, thereby subjecting the intermediaries to certain penalties.

Because of the relative lack of statutory or regulatory guidance or judicial precedent in this area, the foregoing regulatory risks often can be addressed only by approaching applicable insurance regulators with the terms of an insurance derivative transaction to obtain a regulatory determination that the participants are not "conducting an insurance business." While it would be preferable to obtain such determinations regarding broad categories of insurance derivative transactions or structures, many insurance regulators will make such determinations based only on specific facts relating to a particular transaction.

Insurance Securitization

Structural Issues

Insurance securitization represents a relatively recent development in the alternative risk transfer market, although the structural (and conceptual) model for the technique predates its practical emergence in the capital markets.[35] The basic structural model for those insurance securitization transactions that have been successfully accomplished to date is illustrated in figure 4-1:

---

[35] Prior to the emergence of the higher profile insurance securitization transactions in the last several years, the securitization of certain insurance-related risk may have been the subject of certain "one-off" transactions.

Figure 4-1 Basic Insurance Securitization Structure

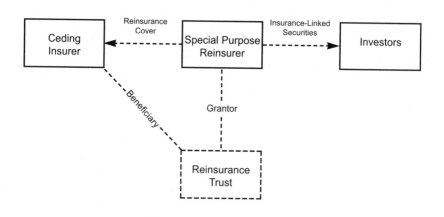

The interests of both the ceding insurer and the investors have a bearing upon the form and structure of the foregoing transaction model. For example, an SPR is typically formed as a vehicle to be inserted between the ceding insurer and the investors to address the legal and regulatory concerns of each party. Although the most direct means by which to transfer insurance risks to the capital markets might be for the ceding insurer to issue insurance-linked securities directly to the investors, the SPR is often necessary because the ceding insurer would not receive the financial statement benefits of traditional reinsurance without the SPR's status as a reinsurance company issuing a reinsurance contract. The SPR also serves as a vehicle in which to insulate the underlying reinsurance premium and the proceeds of the sale of insurance-linked securities from the claims of the ceding insurer's creditors.

While a "special purpose vehicle" is generally formed to facilitate only one transaction, certain practical and administrative reasons related to the basic purposes of an insurance securitization transaction suggest that it may be preferable to use an SPR for multiple simultaneous transactions or to reuse an SPR. For example, because insurance securitization transactions are driven by a ceding insurer's reinsurance coverage needs, which may involve a variety of coverage lines, coverage inception dates, time periods of coverages, and renewals of coverages, a single SPR through which multiple insurance securitization transactions relating to a single ceding insurer flow may be more efficient than establishing a new SPR for each such transaction. One of the concerns of running multiple transactions through a single SPR is that funds relating to one transaction might be subject to unrelated claims. While this concern can be mitigated by having only one ceding insurer's transactions run through the SPR (thereby ensuring that the primary creditor of the SPR as a whole, the ceding insurer, is also the primary creditor of the SPR in each transaction), certain other steps can taken to insulate the funds of one transaction from claims originating from other transactions.

One method to effect such insulation is by contract, whereby all participants in each insurance securitization transaction entered into by the SPR agree to limit their claims to the funds relating to their transaction and to not pursue claims against funds relating to other transactions entered into by the SPR. Alternatively, the SPR could be formed in a jurisdiction, such as the Cayman Islands or Guernsey, which by statute has adopted the concept of the "segregated portfolio" or "cell" company,[36] or in a jurisdiction, such as Bermuda, which permits a similar concept to be effected by a "private act" of the legislature relating solely to the SPR. Generally, in a "segregated portfolio" or "cell" company, the assets and liabilities of one portfolio or cell are insulated from the general assets and liabilities of the company and those relating to another portfolio or cell, and any assets not allocated to a specific portfolio or cell are considered to be general assets of the company.

SPRs are often established in offshore domiciles to take advantage of lower minimum required levels of capital and surplus and the generally reduced level of regulatory scrutiny as compared to U.S.-domiciled insurance companies. The SPR typically is not licensed, qualified, or accredited as an insurance or reinsurance company in any jurisdiction in the United States, and the SPR's business generally is conducted such that it is not selling insurance or reinsurance, or otherwise doing business, in the United States. In this regard, the SPR's officers and representatives will not solicit, advertise, settle claims, or conduct other activities in the

---

[36] See, for example, The Cayman Islands (The Companies (Amendment) (Segregated Portfolio Companies) Law, 1998) and Guernsey (The Protected Cell Companies Ordinance 1997).

United States.[37] The economic efficiency of an offshore SPR also may be enhanced through its minimization of U.S. federal income taxes, depending on the tax characterization of the investment, tax domicile of investors, and other factors.[38]

The ownership of the SPR presents other structural issues. Because the economics of the SPR typically do not involve any material financial opportunity to residual equity holders, ownership of the SPR tends to be driven by regulatory, tax, and other factors. Most offshore domiciles require the SPR to issue some traditional common (voting) equity. Because holders of such equity may be subject to certain financial statement and tax consolidation issues, charitable trusts or other noncommercial persons often will be designated to hold the SPR's equity. Notwithstanding that a particular party may hold statutory equity of the SPR, with respect to U.S. taxpayers, U.S. federal income tax law may characterize all or a portion of an insurance-linked debt security as equity for tax purposes if the SPR's statutory equity is not deemed adequate to "support" such debt. Consequently, an insurance securitization transaction may include tranches of equity or offer units that include an equity component. Alternatively, an insurance securitization transaction may simply provide that the SPR will treat the insurance-linked securities as equity for U.S. federal income tax purposes. While there are a variety of important U.S. and foreign tax issues associated with the ownership of the SPR and other structural aspects of an insurance securitization transaction, such issues are highly fact-specific (depending on the type and tax domicile of the underlying equity holders and investors), and further discussion of these issues is beyond the scope of this chapter.

As noted above, another factor dictating the structure of an insurance securitization transaction is the ceding insurer's desire to receive "credit" for the reinsurance provided by the SPR. In this component of the transaction, the ceding insurer merely is entering into a reinsurance agreement with the SPR. Thus, from an insurance regulatory perspective, this component of the insurance securitization transaction is a typical reinsurance arrangement governed by applicable insurance laws.[39] Because the SPR

---

[37] While the reduced regulatory requirements and level of regulatory scrutiny in non-U.S. jurisdictions are attractive to SPRs as a way to reduce mandated capital and costs of compliance, this reduced level of regulatory scrutiny can be a double-edged sword, as investors will not have the comfort of a comprehensive system of regulatory oversight.

[38] A full analysis of the tax issues with respect to an insurance securitization transaction are essential to the underlying economics, but a discussion of such issues is beyond the scope of this chapter

[39] See section titled "Regulation of Insurance and Reinsurance in the United States."

likely will be neither licensed nor accredited in any U.S. jurisdiction, a "reinsurance trust" for the benefit of the ceding insurer usually is required to enable the ceding insurer to take credit for the reinsurance provided by the SPR. The form and operation of the reinsurance trust will be subject to the insurance laws of the ceding insurer's state of domicile.[40] In addition to the regulatory issues underlying the reinsurance trust, such a structural component also provides a level of financial security to the ceding insurer with respect to its reinsurance premium and any potential claims under the reinsurance agreement, because such amounts are typically held in the reinsurance trust for the primary benefit of the ceding reinsurer.

Securities Regulation

Securities laws apply to insurance securitization transactions because such transactions involve the offer and sale of securities. The securities laws of the jurisdiction in which the SPR is domiciled, as well as the jurisdictions in which the investors are resident and offers to purchase are made, are applicable to the issuance of insurance-linked securities. In the United States, for example, both federal and state securities laws generally require that a registration statement[41] be effective with respect to such securities, unless an applicable exemption exists. Although it would be possible to structure the sale of insurance-linked securities as a registered public offering,[42] such securities are typically offered and sold only

---

[40] See, for example, Section 2D of the NAIC Credit for Reinsurance Model Law, which provides, among other things, that the trust fund must be maintained in a qualified U.S. financial institution, that the assuming insurer must file an annual statement with the commissioner of the ceding insurer's state of domicile and submit to an examination of its books and records, and that the commissioner of the state in which the trust is domiciled (or the commissioner of another state which has accepted principal regulatory oversight of the trust) must approve the trust and any amendments thereto. While the NAIC Credit for Reinsurance Model Law has no force or effect in any state, it is representative of the type of credit for reinsurance regulation found in many states.

[41] Registration would require the issuer of the securities to file a registration statement with the SEC containing certain specified information and to provide disclosure of such information to potential investors. Such information includes risk factors that may affect the securities, use of proceeds of the offering, a description of the issuer's business and legal proceedings in which the issuer is involved, financial statements and a discussion by management relating thereto, and pertinent facts regarding senior management of the issuer. In addition to taking several months to register securities, registration of securities also represents a significant additional expense which would need to be incorporated into the pricing of the reinsurance arrangement and/or the insurance-linked securities.

[42] Prior to successfully consummating its private placement of insurance-linked securities in 1997, Residential Reinsurance Limited (United Services Automobile Association and USAA Casualty Insurance Company) attempted a registered public offering of insurance-linked securities, which ultimately was withdrawn and restructured as a private placement. Winterthur Swiss Insurance Company successfully completed an offering of its principal-protected insurance-linked notes to the Swiss public market in January 1997.

to institutional, fixed-income investors, pursuant to one or more exemptions from registration under the Securities Act. Because of the relatively high-dollar magnitude of most insurance securitization transactions, only two exemptions from registration under the Securities Act typically are available.

First, Section 4(2) of the Securities Act provides that the registration provisions of Section 5 of the Securities Act do not apply to "transactions by an issuer not involving any public offering." Under this section, whether an offering is a "public offering," and thus qualifies for an exemption from registration, is a question of fact, with the burden of proof falling on the party claiming the exemption.[43]

Second, the SEC has created a "safe harbor" under Rule 506 of Regulation D of the Securities Act, which specifies certain requirements and limitations pursuant to which an issuer can obtain greater certainty that the private placement exemption provided by Section 4(2) is available.[44] Yet, while Regulation D provides a safe harbor for an issuer of securities, because such exemption (like the Section 4(2) exemption generally) is only a transaction exemption and not an exemption for the securities themselves, any resale of these exempt securities either must be registered or a separate exemption from registration must apply. Rule 506 creates an exemption for all types of issuers and contains no ceiling on the dollar amount of securities that can be offered. Securities sold pursuant to Rule 506 may be sold to an unlimited number of accredited investors[45] and up to 35 nonaccredited investors. In addition, pursuant to Rule 506(b), each nonaccredited investor generally must qualify as a

---

[43] The U.S. Supreme Court, in *SEC v. Ralston Purina*, 346 U.S.119 (1953), stated that "to be public, an offer need not be open to the whole world." The Court interpreted the Section 4(1) exemption, which was subsequently renumbered as Section 4(2), "in light of its statutory purpose" of "protect[ing] investors by promoting full disclosure of information thought necessary to informed investment decisions." Thus, the Court held that the applicability of the Securities Act turns on whether the offerees need the protection that registration affords them.

[44] Although a private placement pursuant to Regulation D is exempt from registration, the issuer is still required to give notice of the placement to the SEC. This is accomplished by filing a Form D no later than 15 days after the first sale of securities.

[45] Rule 501 defines "accredited investor" as including, among others: (1) any bank, broker or dealer, insurance company, investment company, or certain employee benefit plans; (2) any private business development company; (3) any charitable or educational organization with total assets greater than $5 million; (4) any director, executive officer, or general partner of the issuer; (5) any person with a net worth or joint net worth with a spouse of more than $1 million; (6) any person with an annual income of more than $200,000 or together with a spouse more than $300,000; (7) any trust with more than $5 million in assets which is managed by a "sophisticated" person; and (8) any entity in which all of the equity owners are accredited investors.

sophisticated investor.[46] Finally, information regarding the securities, the issuer, and other aspects of the offering must be furnished to all nonaccredited investors,[47] and no general solicitation or advertising may be made concerning the offering.

Regardless of whether registration of the insurance-linked securities is required or an exemption from registration is available, the "antifraud" provisions of the Securities Act will apply.[48] Generally, the antifraud provisions of the Securities Act impose civil liability on any person who offers or sells a security, by means of written or oral communication, which includes "an untrue statement of a material fact or omits to state a material fact necessary in order to make the statements . . . not misleading."[49] Consequently, the registration statement or private placement memorandum distributed in connection with the offering of insurance-linked securities must contain information necessary to allow an investor to make an informed investment decision. The disclosure documents typically describe the securities, the SPR and its business operations, the use of proceeds of the offering, tax information, and other relevant information. The distributed material will also describe "risk factors," or "investment considerations," which should be considered by prospective investors. In addition to typical risk factors relating to debt securities, the disclosure material in insurance securitization transactions will describe risk factors unique to insurance-linked securities, such as the risk of loss of principal or interest due to factors other than credit exposure, the risk that the date of maturity of the securities will be extended, the unpredictability of risk relating to catastrophes or other insurance-related events, risks relating to investing in an entity domiciled in a foreign jurisdiction, and the risk that the investor could be subject to insurance laws. Also unique to offerings of insurance-linked securities, the disclosure documents often include extensive historical information relating to the

---

[46] Rule 506(b)(2)(ii) states that a sophisticated investor is a "purchaser who is not an accredited investor either alone or with his purchaser representative(s) [but] has such knowledge and experience in financial and business matters that he is capable of evaluating the merits and risks of the prospective investment, or the issuer reasonably believes immediately prior to making any sale that such purchaser comes within this description." A purchaser representative is defined in Rule 501, in part, as a person who "has such knowledge and experience in financial and business matters that he is capable of evaluating, alone, or together with other purchaser representatives of the purchaser, or together with the purchaser, the merits and risks of the prospective investment."

[47] Rule 502(b)(2) provides the type and scope of information to be provided, based on the relative size of the offering. With respect to offerings over $7,500,000, the information to be provided is similar to that included in a registration statement filed under the Securities Act.

[48] See Sections 12(a)(2) and 17(a) of the Securities Act and Section 10 of the Securities Exchange Act and Rule 10b-5 promulgated thereunder.

[49] See Section 12(a)(2) of the Securities Act and Rule 10b-5 under the Securities Exchange Act.

underlying risk triggers (e.g., hurricanes or earthquakes), as well as data developed by event modeling firms to estimate losses that may be expected to result from the occurrence of these risk triggers during the term of the insurance-linked securities.

Resale of Unregistered Securities

As noted above, any resales of securities issued in a private placement must either be registered or independently qualify for an applicable exemption. Rule 144A of the Securities Act provides a safe harbor from the registration requirement for resales of unregistered securities made to "qualified institutional buyers" (QIBs). To qualify for this safe harbor, the following four requirements must be met: (i) the resale may be made only to QIBs,[50] (ii) the purchaser must be aware of the seller's reliance on Rule 144A,[51] (iii) the securities to be resold must not be of the same class as a security publicly traded in the United States,[52] and (iv) current information about the issuer must be available.[53]

---

[50] Rule 144A allows unlimited resales of any eligible security of any issuer to purchasers that the seller of the securities reasonably believes are QIBs. QIBs include: (i) an institution, other than a registered broker/dealer, that owns and invests on a discretionary basis at least $100 million in securities of companies not affiliated with the institution, or is reasonably believed by the seller to be such an institution; (ii) a registered broker/dealer that owns and invests on a discretionary basis at least $10 million in securities of issuers not affiliated with such broker/dealer, or a registered broker/dealer who, regardless of the amount of securities owned, acts in "riskless principal transactions" on behalf of QIBs; and (iii) a bank or savings and loan association that owns and invests on a discretionary basis at least $100 million in securities and has an audited net worth of at least $25 million.

[51] Because investors who purchase unregistered securities in a Rule 144A resale can themselves resell only pursuant to Rule 144A or another available exemption from registration, the 144A seller must take reasonable steps to ensure that the purchaser is aware that the seller is relying on 144A to sell the securities. Although there is no clear guidance from the SEC as to the meaning of "reasonable steps," sellers generally satisfy this requirement by obtaining a written acknowledgement from the purchaser indicating awareness that the seller is relying on Rule 144A.

[52] Rule 144A is available for the resale of any domestic or foreign security unless the security is one that, when issued, is of the same class as a security listed on a U.S. national securities exchange or quoted in a U.S. automated interdealer quotation system such as NASDAQ. Not only does this requirement prevent the creation of dual markets, but it also prevents these securities, which were issued with limited disclosure, from falling into the hands of public investors.

[53] Rule 144A provides that where the resale involves the securities of an issuer that is neither subject to the periodic reporting requirements of the Securities Exchange Act, nor a foreign company exempt from such requirements pursuant to Rule 12g3-2(b), the issuer must make certain basic information available to all holders of outstanding Rule 144A securities and any prospective purchasers of such securities designated by a holder. The information to be delivered must be reasonably current as of the date of any resale of a Rule 144A security and must include (i) a brief statement of the nature of the issuer's businesses, products, and services offered, and (ii) the issuer's most recent balance sheet, profit-and-loss and retained earnings statements, and similar financial statements for such part of the two preceding fiscal years that the issuer has been in operation.

If sales of the insurance-linked securities will occur outside of the United States, Regulation S of the Securities Act may apply, which, in general, exempts from registration offers and sales of securities that occur "outside the United States." Depending upon the contractual arrangements, if any, between the issuer and the securities' intermediaries, the exemption may be obtained under Rule 903(c)(i) under the Securities Act (securities of foreign issuers) or Rule 904 under the Securities Act (resales).

If the contractual arrangements between the issuer and the intermediary are such that the intermediary is a "distributor"[54] of the securities under Regulation S, Rule 903(c)(i) would apply. Under Rule 903(c)(i), an unregistered offer or sale of securities of a foreign issuer may be made with no conditions other than (i) the offer or sale is an "offshore transaction," (ii) no "directed selling efforts" are made in the United States, and (iii) the issuer reasonably believes that there is no substantial U.S. market interest in the class of securities to be sold. An offer and sale of securities is an "offshore transaction" if (a) the offer is not made to a person in the United States and (b) the buyer is outside the United States or the seller and any person acting on its behalf reasonably believe that the buyer is outside the United States.

If the contractual arrangements between the issuer and the securities intermediary do not result in the intermediary being a "distributor" of the securities, Rule 904, the resale provision of Regulation S, may provide an exemption. Rule 904 provides that resales are deemed to occur "outside the United States" and are thereby exempt from registration if, among other things,[55] (i) the offer or sale is made in an "offshore transaction"

---

[54] Section 902(c) of the Securities Act defines "distributor" as "any underwriter, dealer, or other person who participates, pursuant to a contractual arrangement, in the distribution of the securities offered or sold in reliance on . . . Regulation S."

[55] The other conditions in Rule 904 relate to selling commissions and directed selling efforts in the United States.

and (ii) neither the seller nor any person acting on his behalf knows that the buyer is a "U.S. person."[56]

The Investment Companies Act of 1940

In addition to the securities laws discussed above, an issuer of insurance-linked securities should also determine whether the Investment Companies Act of 1940 (1940 Act) will have any effect on the transaction. Section 3(a)(1) of the 1940 Act broadly defines the term "investment company" such that it arguably could include a typical issuer of insurance-linked securities.[57]

Notwithstanding this broad definition, the 1940 Act and its rules provide for exceptions from the definition of "investment company" for U.S. insurance companies (Section 3(c)(3)), U.S. insurance holding companies (Section 3(c)(6)), non-U.S. insurance companies (Rule 3a-6), and non-U.S. insurance holding companies (Rule 3a-1). Rule 3a-6, for example, which would be the operative provision for an offshore SPR, defines a "foreign insurance company" as "an insurance company incorporated or organized under the laws of a country other than the United States, or a

---

[56] "U.S. person" means:
  (i)   Any natural person resident in the United States;
  (ii) Any partnership or corporation organized or incorporated under the laws of the United States;
  (iii) Any estate of which any executor or administrator is a U.S. person;
  (iv) Any trust of which any trustee is a U.S. person;
  (v)   Any agency or branch of a foreign entity located in the United States;
  (vi) Any nondiscretionary account or similar account (other than an estate or trust) held by a dealer or other fiduciary for the benefit or account of a U.S. person;
  (vii) Any discretionary account or similar account (other than an estate or trust) held by a dealer or other fiduciary organized, incorporated, or (if an individual) resident in the United States; and
  (viii) Any partnership or corporation if: (a) organized or incorporated under the laws of any non-United States jurisdiction; and (b) formed by a U.S. person principally for the purpose of investing in securities not registered under the Securities Act, unless it is organized or incorporated, and owned, by accredited investors (as defined in Rule 501(a) under the Securities Act) who are not natural persons, estates, or trusts.

[57] Under Section 3(a)(1) of the 1940 Act, an "investment company" is defined as any issuer which:
  (a)   is or holds itself out as being engaged primarily, or proposes to engage primarily, in the business of investing, reinvesting, or trading in securities;
  (b)   is engaged or proposes to engage in the business of issuing face-amount certificates of the installment type, or has been engaged in such business and has any such certificate outstanding; or
  (c)   is engaged or proposes to engage in the business of investing, reinvesting, owning, holding, or trading in securities, and owns or proposes to acquire investment securities having a value exceeding 40 percent of the value of such issuer's total assets (exclusive of government securities and cash items) on an unconsolidated basis.

political subdivision of a country other than the United States, that is: (i) regulated as such by that country's or subdivision's government or any agency thereof; (ii) engaged primarily and predominantly in (A) the writing of insurance agreements of the type specified in section 3(a)(8) of the Securities Act of 1933 . . ., except for the substitution of supervision by foreign government insurance regulators for the regulators referred to in that section; or (B) the reinsurance of risks on such agreements underwritten by insurance companies; and (iii) not operated for the purpose of evading the provisions of the [1940] Act."[58]

If an issuer of insurance-linked securities falls within the definition of a "foreign insurance company" under the 1940 Act, such entity will be excepted from the definition of an "investment company" and not subject to regulation under the 1940 Act. This definition does not include, however, a separate account or other pool of assets organized in the form of a trust or otherwise in which interests are separately offered. Consequently, it is unclear whether the insurance company exceptions would apply to "segregated portfolios" or "cells."

A foreign issuer of insurance-linked securities which does not fall within the Rule 3a-6 definition of a foreign insurance company may nevertheless be excepted from the definition of an "investment company" by complying with either Section 3(c)(1) or 3(c)(7) of the 1940 Act, both of which are exceptions for issuers engaging in certain private placements of securities. Section 3(c)(1) excepts from the definition of an "investment company" a private placement of securities made to 100 persons or less, while Section 3(c)(7) excepts a private placement of securities made to "qualified purchasers."[59]

---

[58] A foreign insurance company relying on Rule 3a-6 for exemption from the Act may be required to file Form F-N with the SEC in connection with the filing of a registration statement (i.e., a public offering) under the Securities Act.

[59] An issuer of insurance-linked securities relying on either the Section 3(c)(1) or Section 3(c)(7) exception from the definition of an "investment company" would still be deemed to be an investment company for the purposes of certain investment limitations.

Section 2(a)(51)(A) of the 1940 Act defines a "qualified purchaser" as: (i) any natural person with $5,000,000 or more in investments, (ii) any company with $5,000,000 or more in investments that is owned directly or indirectly by or for two or more natural persons who are related as siblings or spouse (including former spouses), or direct lineal descendants by birth or adoption, spouses of such persons, the estates of such persons, or foundations, charitable organizations, or trusts established by or for the benefit of such persons, (iii) any trust that was not formed for the specific purpose of acquiring the securities offered to which the trustee and each person who contributes assets to the trust is a qualified purchaser under (i), (ii) or (iv), and (iv) any person, acting for its own account or the accounts of other qualified purchasers, who in the aggregate owns and invests on a discretionary basis, not less than $25,000,000 in investments.

Regulation of Brokers, Dealers, and Investment Advisers

While the issuer of insurance-linked securities must be concerned with securities-related regulation, those who effect transactions in, or advise on the purchase of, these securities also may be subject to extensive regulation. In this regard, an underwriter, selling agent, or other intermediary involved in buying or selling insurance-linked securities may be subject to broker/dealer regulation.

The regulation of "brokers" and "dealers" is two-tiered—brokers and dealers are regulated by both the SEC and their own mandatory self-regulatory association. Section 3(24) of the Securities Exchange Act defines a "broker" as "any person engaged in the business of effecting transactions in securities for the account of others." A dealer is defined in Section 3(25) as "any person engaged in the business of buying and selling securities for his own account, through a broker or otherwise."[60] Under Section 15(a) of the Securities Exchange Act, a broker or dealer is prohibited from using any instrumentality of interstate commerce to effect any transaction in securities without being registered with the SEC.

In addition to being registered with the SEC, pursuant to Section 15(b)(8) of the Securities Exchange Act, all broker/dealers must also be members of a securities association. Currently, the National Association of Securities Dealers (NASD) is the only such association, and it is subject to the specific oversight of the SEC. As part of its system of regulating broker/dealers, the NASD has promulgated Rules of Conduct which cover nearly every aspect of a broker/dealer's business. Some of the issues covered by the Rules of Conduct include the suitability of investments for clients, as well as the appropriate amount of commissions and "mark-ups" for broker/dealers on the sale of securities.

An individual or entity that advises an investor, such as a hedge fund, with respect to investments in insurance-linked securities may be subject to regulation as an investment adviser. Like the activities of broker/dealers, the activities of investment advisers are also regulated by the SEC. Investment advisers are regulated under the Investment Advisers Act of 1940 (Investment Advisers Act). The Investment Advisers Act defines the term "investment adviser" as:

---

[60] The term "dealer" "does not include a bank or any person buying or selling securities for his own account, either individually or in some fiduciary capacity, but not as part of a regular business."

any person who, for compensation, engages in the business of advising others, either directly or through publications or writings, as to the value of securities or as to the advisability of investing in, purchasing, or selling securities, or who for compensation and as a part of a regular business, issues or promulgates analyses or reports concerning securities.

In addition, the definition specifically excludes a bank or bank holding company which is not an investment company, professionals (including broker/dealers) whose performance of advisory services is incidental to their professions, publishers of general and regular circulation publications, and "some analysts limiting their focus to certain obligations which are exempt as direct obligations of or guaranteed by the United States." Section 203(a) of the Investment Advisers Act requires any investment adviser using an instrumentality of interstate commerce in connection with its business to be registered.[61] Under Section 203A(a)(1), an investment adviser required to be registered with the state in which its principal place of business is located is required to be registered with the SEC, in addition to being registered with the state, only if the adviser[62] (i) has assets under management[63] of $25,000,000 or more, or (ii) advises a registered investment company. If an investment adviser's home state does not require registration, the investment adviser will be required to register with the SEC, regardless of the foregoing standards.

---

[61] Section 203(b) provides the following exemptions to the registration requirement of Section 203(a): (i) advisers whose only clients are located in the adviser's principal state of business and who do not give advice regarding securities listed or admitted to unlisted trading privileges on any national securities exchange, (ii) advisers whose only clients are insurance companies, and (iii) persons who are not advisers under the 1940 Act. This third category includes any adviser who has had fewer than 15 clients in the 12 preceding months and who does not represent to the public that he or she is an investment adviser nor acts as an investment adviser to a registered investment company or a business development company.

[62] Under Section 203A(c), the SEC may permit registration with the SEC in other situations where the application of this section would be unfair or a burden on interstate commerce.

[63] Section 203A(a)(2) defines "assets under management" as "the securities portfolios with respect to which an investment adviser provides continuous and regular supervisory or management services."

Insurance Regulation

While issuers, broker/dealers, and investment advisers involved with insurance-linked securities must comply with applicable securities laws, investors generally consider themselves to be the beneficiaries of, and not subject to, these and other regulations. Nevertheless, it is conceivable that investors in insurance-linked instruments could be considered to be "conducting an insurance business," by virtue of their assuming risk that traditionally is the subject of insurance. If an investor were deemed to be conducting an insurance business, that investor could be found to be operating without being appropriately licensed, authorized, or qualified as an insurance company. Similarly, an underwriter, selling agent, or broker/dealer deemed to be conducting an insurance agency, brokerage, or intermediary business by virtue of its role in an insurance securitization transaction could be found to be operating without being appropriately licensed as an insurance or reinsurance agent, broker, or intermediary.

The risk to an investor of being subject to insurance regulation should be adequately described in the insurance securitization transaction's registration statement or private placement memorandum. Although there is some limited regulatory and judicial guidance regarding the definition of the "business of insurance" and its related regulatory effect, at the present time, such guidance is insufficient to allow attorneys to opine that an investor would not be deemed to be conducting an insurance business in connection with typical insurance securitization transactions. Due to the relative lack of legal and regulatory precedent, the most effective way to address this regulatory issue, and the corresponding risk to underwriters, selling agents, and broker/dealers, may be to approach insurance regulators in all relevant jurisdictions in an effort to obtain "no action"-type determinations that the participants in the insurance securitization transaction are not "conducting an insurance business." While a general, categorical determination would be beneficial, regulators may be hesitant to provide such a general conclusion because of the highly fact- and structure-specific nature of the transactions and the relative novelty of insurance securitizations in general. An insurance regulator may be more likely to provide comfort that insurance securitization participants are not conducting an insurance business in the context of a specific transaction.

In this regard, underwriters, selling agents, and/or broker/dealers involved in several recent insurance securitization transactions have sought regulatory determinations from applicable jurisdictions with respect to the terms and structure of the underlying transaction. These requests have sought a determination that the participants will not be deemed by the applicable insurance regulators to be conducting an insurance business or insurance agency, brokerage, or intermediary business in the subject jurisdiction.[64] To mitigate potential insurance regulatory exposure, the plans of offering regarding insurance-linked securities have limited the offerees and other participants to those governed by jurisdictions which have determined that such participants will not be deemed to be conducting an insurance business. Until specific statutory guidance is adopted or more broadly applicable common law or regulatory assurances are available, the foregoing procedures and limitations on the plan of offering may be the only practical approach for resolving the underlying insurance regulatory issues.

U.S. Insurance Companies' Use of Insurance Derivatives and Securitization

The development of insurance derivative and securitization products has provided the insurance industry with additional methods by which to transfer risk, as well as additional asset classes in which to invest. In this regard, it is necessary to determine whether an insurance company is authorized to engage in insurance derivative and securitization transactions. With respect to insurance derivative transactions, an insurance company may be on either side of the transaction—transferring risk or assuming risk. To the extent that an insurance company is transferring risk through insurance derivatives, such a transaction would probably be viewed as a hedge of its insurance liabilities and subject to corresponding regulation. Conversely, an insurance company seeking to assume risk through the use of insurance derivatives will probably be considered to be engaging in a speculative transaction, regulated as an investment or investment practice under applicable law. With respect to an insurance securitization transaction, there is little question that an insurance company has the authority to cede insurance risk to a properly structured SPR pursuant to a reinsurance agreement. If an insurance company seeks to invest in insurance-linked securities, the existence and extent of such authority will be governed by applicable insurance company investment

---

[64] While applicable insurance regulators generally have been cooperative in responding to such requests, any such determination (whether or not it concludes that the participants are not conducting an insurance business) will not necessarily be binding upon any court or third party that may challenge such determination.

laws. A corollary issue is the financial statement reporting and risk-based capital implications of an insurer's use of insurance derivative and securitization products.

U.S. Insurance Companies' Use of Insurance Derivatives

Only California,[65] Illinois,[66] and New York[67] have expressly addressed an insurance company's authority to engage directly in exchange-traded (e.g., CBOT) insurance derivatives. In each of these jurisdictions, such authority has been limited to hedging transactions.[68]

With respect to OTC insurance derivatives, the authors are not aware of any state insurance code that expressly contemplates this category of insurance derivatives.[69] Consequently, the analysis of an insurance company's authority to engage in OTC insurance derivative transactions should initially focus on the insurance company's authority to engage in general OTC derivative transactions. In this regard, few state insurance codes provide clear authority for an insurance company to engage in OTC

---

[65] Section 1212 of the California Insurance Code authorizes domestic incorporated insurers to invest, in bona fide hedging transactions, in insurance futures contracts (and call options thereon) that "have attained an average daily trading volume of at least 250 contracts and an open interest of 1,000 contracts as reported by the relevant board of trade for the one-month period prior to the insurer initiating the transaction." This authorization requires that, among other limitations, the insurer meet certain aggregate capital and surplus requirements and that the futures contracts be exchange-traded.

[66] Section 126.2HH of the Illinois Insurance Code (the "Illinois Code") defines the term "future" to expressly include an insurance future, and Section 126.2V(2) of the Illinois Code, in turn, includes futures in its definition of "derivative instruments." Thus, under Sections 126.18 and 126.31, which authorize Illinois-domiciled life and health insurers and property and casualty insurers, respectively, to engage in derivative transactions, an Illinois insurer may use insurance futures to engage in hedging transactions (and income generation transactions), subject to certain limitations.

[67] Until its "sunset" on December 31, 1996, Section 1403(c)(8) of the New York Insurance Code authorized New York domestic insurers to enter "into bona fide hedging transactions with respect to insurance liabilities by buying insurance futures contracts" and call options on such contracts, subject to the requirements of such section. The underlying bill was provisionally passed for a period of three years; the section "sunset" on December 31, 1996, without further action.

[68] While insurance company authority has been limited to hedging purposes, other nonregulated parties may be authorized to engage in exchange-traded insurance derivative transactions for speculative purposes.

[69] Notwithstanding (i) an insurance company's authority to engage in exchange-traded and OTC insurance derivative transactions and (ii) the characterization and reporting of such transactions, derivatives strategies (with respect to both transferring and assuming risk) may be utilized by other members of the insurer's holding company system to achieve the desired result on a consolidated basis.

derivative transactions.[70] Regardless of the lack of definitive statutory guidance, most states have taken some official or unofficial position on domestic insurance company use of OTC derivative instruments. Generally, such positions involve the application of basket/leeway clauses[71] or other existing provisions to specific derivative instruments used for hedging purposes, with a corresponding express or implied prohibition against transactions of a speculative nature.[72] In many instances, underlying statutory provisions were originally adopted without any contemplation of specific derivative instruments or the existence of an OTC derivatives market. Similarly, even where the regulation of OTC derivatives is more developed, such regulation generally has not contemplated the emergence of insurance derivatives.[73]

Insurance companies which engage in insurance futures and insurance futures options transactions must report such transactions on Schedule DC of their statutory financial statements. While Schedule DC of the NAIC annual statement blank originally was added to report insurance futures and insurance futures options traded on the CBOT, other transactions encompassed within the definitions provided in the NAIC Annual Statement Instructions could be subject to reporting on that Schedule.[74]

---

[70] The following are examples of statutes which provide clear authority for an insurance company to engage in OTC derivative transactions: Section 1191.5 of the California Insurance Code (authorization for life insurers only), Sections 126.18 and 126.31 of the Illinois Insurance Code, and Section 1403(d)(2)(A) and (d)(7)(A) of the New York Insurance Code. (Note: As this book went to press, certain revisions to the New York Insurance Code regarding derivatives were passed by the New York legislature, but were not yet signed into law.)

[71] The "basket/leeway clause" is a term used to refer to the provision of a state's investment law which authorizes an insurance company to invest a limited portion of its assets in instruments which are not otherwise specifically identified in the investment law or which exceed the quantitative limitations applicable to a specified category of investments.

[72] See, for example, Sections 126.18A(1) and 126.31A(1) of the Illinois Insurance Code, Section 44-5149 of the Nebraska Insurance Code, Section 1403(d)(2)(A) of the New York Insurance Code, and Regulation 142 of the New York Insurance Regulations. (Note: As this book went to press, certain revisions to the New York Insurance Code regarding derivatives were passed by the New York legislature, but were not yet signed into law.)

[73] Such regulation typically contemplates the hedging of traditional financial risk through the use of derivatives. It is unclear whether the hedging of non-investment-related exposures, such as insurance risk, would be authorized.

[74] An "insurance futures contract" to be reported on Schedule DC is "a futures contract based on an underlying index or performance of insurance contracts (policies) or factors relating thereto, or such other definition as may be specified under the statutes, regulations and administrative rulings of a particular state." An "insurance futures option" to be reported on Schedule DC is "a put or call option on an Insurance Futures contract." NAIC Annual Statement Instructions (1997), p. 261 (Life, Accident and Health) and p. 182 (Property and Casualty).

All derivative instruments (other than insurance futures and options on insurance futures, which should be reported on Schedule DC) to which a U.S. insurer is a party must be reported on Schedule DB of the annual statement. Schedule DB requires the disclosure of a variety of information with respect to a given derivative transaction. It specifically applies to options (other than Schedule DC options), caps, floors, collars, swaps, forwards, and futures (other than Schedule DC futures).

U.S. Insurance Companies' Use of Insurance Securitization Transactions

Authority to Transfer Risk

The authority of an insurance company to use insurance securitization transactions is not a significant U.S. insurance regulatory issue, because the subject insurance company typically will cede its risk to an SPR pursuant to a reinsurance agreement. Consequently, the only necessary authority relates to the ceding insurer's authority to cede reinsurance and to receive a benefit therefor on its statutory financial statements. That authority is well established in all U.S. jurisdictions.[75]

Authority to Invest in Insurance-Linked Securities

The insurance industry also has expressed an appetite on the "buy-side" of the emerging insurance securitization market. In this regard, insurance companies, particularly life insurers, have begun to explore the benefits of investing in insurance-linked securities as an alternative asset class with little correlation to the characteristics and general risk profile of the remainder of its assets and liabilities. In response to this interest, insurance regulators have begun to develop the regulatory parameters and reporting models pursuant to which insurance companies may invest in insurance-linked securities.

No U.S. state insurance code currently provides express authority for an insurance company to invest in insurance-linked securities. Consequently, in determining whether an insurance company is authorized to invest in insurance-linked securities (other than pursuant to an

---

[75] See section titled "Regulation of Insurance and Reinsurance in the United States." While a particular jurisdiction could regulate the cession of risk to an SPR which is the subject of a securitization transaction, such a regulatory approach seems unlikely because of the existing regulatory scheme applied to the underlying reinsurance transaction. The authors are unaware of any jurisdiction that has identified this side of the emerging securitization market as an area of concern.

applicable basket/leeway clause), the insurance company must identify an authorized category of investments under which insurance-linked securities may qualify. Most U.S. state insurance company investment regulatory schemes respect the basic form of an investment security, and, although insurance-linked securities may have certain unique characteristics, including the risk of principal invasion, such instruments typically are structured as debt instruments. Because U.S. state insurance laws currently do not contemplate insurance-linked securities, such securities generally would qualify as "obligations" or "evidences of indebtedness" under most current state insurance codes, thereby providing insurance companies with potentially broad authority to invest in insurance-linked securities. Of course, certain qualitative and quantitative limitations will apply, including limitations relating to the rating of such securities by the SVO.[76]

Under the NAIC Model Investment Law, principal-protected insurance-linked securities are treated as "rated credit instruments."[77] With respect to non-principal-protected insurance-linked securities, the NAIC takes the position that such securities should be treated as "special rated

---

[76] See section titled "SVO Ratings, Statutory Reporting, and Risk-Based Capital."

[77] Section 2.RRR(1) of the NAIC Model Investment Law defines the term "rated credit instruments" to mean a contractual right to receive cash or another rated credit instrument from another entity which instrument:

    (a)   Is rated or required to be rated by the SVO;
    (b)   In the case of an instrument with a maturity of 397 days or less, is issued, guaranteed or insured by an entity that is rated by, or another obligation of such entity is rated by, the SVO or by a nationally recognized statistical rating organization recognized by the SVO;
    (c)   In the case of an instrument with a maturity of 90 days or less is issued by a qualified bank;
    (d)   Is a share of a class one bond mutual fund; or
    (e)   Is a share of a money market mutual fund.

However, pursuant to Section 2.RRR(2), "rated credit instrument" does not mean:

    (a)   An instrument that is mandatorily, or at the option of the issuer, convertible to an equity interest; or
    (b)   A security that has a par value and whose terms provide that the issuer's net obligation to repay all or part of the security's par value is determined by reference to the performance of an equity, a commodity, a foreign currency, or an index of equities, commodities, foreign currencies, or combinations thereof.

credit instruments" under the NAIC Model Investment Law,[78] subject to more stringent quantitative investment limitations. Of course, the Model Investment Law is of no official force or effect unless adopted by an applicable state legislature.[79]

SVO Ratings, Statutory Reporting, and Risk-Based Capital

An insurer's authority to invest in insurance-linked securities is separate from the treatment of such securities for statutory reporting and risk-based capital purposes. The NAIC typically determines how a particular category of assets will be treated for statutory reporting and risk-based capital purposes. In this regard, although state legislatures have not yet adopted insurance company investment provisions that specifically address insurance-linked securities, the NAIC has already developed a framework pursuant to which insurance companies must report and value investments in insurance-linked securities. This framework focuses primarily on the issue of "principal-protection" (i.e., whether the terms of the securities provide for the unconditional return of all principal to the security holder). In this regard, the NAIC has determined that principal-protected insurance-linked securities may be treated as bonds for statutory reporting and risk-based capital purposes, and the SVO may rate such securities accordingly.

In light of the lack of specific regulation limiting the authority of insurance companies to invest in non-principal-protected insurance-linked securities, and the practical inability of the SVO to rate these

---

[78] Section 2.CCCC of the NAIC Model Investment Law defines a "special rated credit instrument" as "an instrument that is structured so that, if it is held until retired by or on behalf of the issuer, its rate of return, based on its purchase cost and any cash flow stream possible under the structure of the transaction, may become negative due to reasons other than the credit risk associated with the issuer of the instrument." However, this section further states that a "rated credit instrument" is not a "special rated credit instrument" if it is one of an enumerated list of instruments, which includes "an instrument, other than an asset-backed security, that has a par value and is purchased at a price no greater than one hundred ten percent (110%) of par." While this exemptive language would appear to encompass most forms of insurance-linked securities, thereby avoiding categorization as "special rated credit instruments," the NAIC and Illinois insurance regulators take the position that non-principal-protected insurance-linked securities should be treated as "special rated credit instruments" instead of "rated credit instruments."

[79] According to the NAIC, as of August 1998, only Illinois has adopted an investment law (Section 126.1 *et seq.* of the Illinois Insurance Code) similar to the NAIC Model Investment Law.

securities,[80] the NAIC has determined that such securities generally should be treated as equity for statutory reporting and risk-based capital purposes. In the fall of 1997, however, the NAIC Financial Condition Subcommittee adopted a report from its Valuation of Securities Task Force to allow the SVO to treat certain non-principal-protected insurance-linked securities as bonds. Specifically, the NAIC determined that non-principal-protected natural catastrophe-linked bonds (i.e., return of principal linked to the occurrence or nonoccurrence of a natural event, such as a hurricane, an earthquake, or a flood) which are rated and monitored by a nationally recognized statistical rating organization (e.g., Standard & Poor's Rating Group, Moody's Investors Services Inc., Fitch Investors Service, or Duff & Phelps Credit Rating Co.) could be treated as bonds by the SVO.[81] Additionally, a rating organization's rating of these securities may be adopted by the SVO, thereby providing an SVO rating to non-principal-protected insurance-linked securities.

Effective December 31, 1997, this approach was codified as Part Seven, Section 4(c) of the Purposes and Procedures Manual of the NAIC Securities Valuation Office. Consequently, principal-protected insurance-linked securities and this limited category of non-principal-protected insurance-linked securities may be reported on Schedule D of an insurance company's statutory financial statements. Any other insurance-linked security must be reported as "equity" on Schedule BA of an insurance company's statutory financial statements. Thus, even if an insurance company is authorized by its applicable state insurance code to invest in non-principal-protected insurance-linked securities as "obligations" or "evidences of indebtedness," the company presumably must report such securities as "equity" on Schedule BA of its statutory financial statements, pursuant to the rules of the NAIC.

---

[80] In a June 16, 1997, conference call of the Invested Asset Working Group of the NAIC Valuation of Securities Task Force, a representative of the SVO indicated that the SVO did not have, nor did it expect to ever have, the expertise to judge the appropriateness of the modeling applied to many insurance-linked securitization transactions that would be necessary to rate certain insurance-linked securities. In this regard, the representative indicated that, if the SVO were required to rate such securities, it would have to rely completely on the nationally recognized statistical rating organizations for such expertise.

[81] See Minutes of the NAIC Financial Condition Subcommittee, September 24, 1997, 1:00 p.m., adopting the report of the Valuation of Securities Task Force, as set forth in the Minutes of the Valuation of Securities Task Force, September 23, 1997, 11:30 a.m.

If an insurance-linked security is reported as "equity" on Schedule BA, it will receive the risk-based capital charge applicable to Schedule BA assets,[82] which would be comparatively higher than the charge associated with the same insurance-linked security if treated as a debt instrument. Depending on its maturity, an insurance-linked security treated as a debt instrument by the SVO would be reported on Schedule D of the insurance company's statutory financial statements and would receive the risk-based capital charge applicable to similarly rated bonds.

*****

Note: The authors would like to acknowledge the contributions of their colleagues Michael M. Philipp (associate-Financial Services) and Marguerite M. Elias (partner-Corporate/Securities).

---

[82] See NAIC Risk-Based Capital Report Including Overview and Instructions for Companies (separate instructions for life and property and casualty companies).

Part II
The (Old and New)
Market Players

Insurance Firms' New Edge: Capital Market Ventures

Bernard L. Hengesbaugh
CNA

When the Chicago Board of Trade moved to put together a securitized insurance product in the early 1990s, many of us in the insurance industry didn't really want securitization to happen. Reinsurers weren't too excited about an idea that could bring down prices for catastrophe reinsurance. Insurers weren't sure securitization would help much either.

Today, securitization is regarded as one of the most exciting ideas in the insurance industry. Many insurance groups, including CNA, are launching securitization ventures. What changed?

The major change is the awareness that securitization is coming, with or without the participation of any particular insurance organization. Securitization will expand the range of risk management options for our customers. Insurance leaders thus have two choices—get in front of the trend or get run over by it.

The insurance industry's attitude shift is an important turning point in the evolution of insurance securitization. This chapter will explore that evolutionary process, then take a closer look at the CNA securitization venture, Hedge Financial Products, Inc. Finally, the chapter will discuss the challenges facing the insurance securitization business as a whole.

Evolution of Insurance Securitization

Other contributors to this book have addressed major drivers of insurance securitization. Quite simply, a mismatch exists between the magnitude of property loss exposures worldwide and insurance capacity to finance these risks. There are also changes in customer demand. Increasingly, larger corporate customers are looking for risk management services on a very broad basis—beyond the limits of traditional insurance products.

In addition to these evolutionary drivers, insurance securitization reflects changes in the basic character of our industry. Insurance is becoming much more of a rough-and-tumble, entrepreneurial business. Boundaries between traditional lines of insurance are blurring. Different segments of the business are crossing into each other's traditional turf. As a result, insurance is becoming a business of alliances and partnerships, where a partner one day becomes a competitor the next.

Looking beneath the surface of these changes, we see the insurance industry being restructured on three levels: financial restructuring, consolidation, and liability restructuring. Securitization reflects this restructuring at each level.

Financial restructuring refers to changes in the sources of capital that back insurance organizations. Traditionally, these sources have had a long-term orientation: policyholders of mutual companies interested in stable protection over time and shareholders of stock companies interested in long-term appreciation. In the past few years, however, we have seen a shift toward investment groups such as Trident, Insurance Partners, and Kohlberg Kravis Roberts (KKR). These groups target firms for acquisition and seek an active role in managing the business. Their objective is a relatively short-term return on investment, versus the longer-term orientation of traditional investors. KKR exemplified this approach in 1996 with its sale of American Re to Munich Re. KKR realized a $1.7 billion profit, an annualized return of more than 60 percent since buying American Re four years earlier from Aetna. The bottom line of financial restructuring is that a new class of investors is bringing an investment banking-oriented business agenda to the insurance industry. In a similar fashion, securitization is bringing investment banking and insurance closer together.

Consolidation restructuring refers to the merger and acquisition activity over the past few years. The merger of CNA and Continental, the Travelers acquisition of the property/casualty operations of Aetna, and the acquisition of American States by Safeco exemplify this level of restructuring. On the insurance brokerage side, the mergers of Aon and Alexander & Alexander and of Marsh & McLennan and Johnson &

Higgins show the same forces at work. Over time, this restructuring will result in an industry of stronger, more efficient organizations, better able to respond to risks faced by their customers. Securitization has similar objectives: managing risk in ways and at levels the industry cannot accommodate at present.

The third level of restructuring concerns liabilities. Examples of liability restructuring include the reconstruction of Lloyd's of London and Cigna's proposed restructuring to wall off the massive asbestos and environmental liabilities attached to its old business. These transactions involve dividing the liabilities of an entity and supporting the restructured liabilities with separate asset pools. By doing so, insurance organizations are tapping new approaches to dealing with huge past liabilities. Similarly, securitization provides a new approach to supporting the huge exposures to future catastrophes.

From a broad perspective, then, securitization is just one more sign of a rapidly restructuring industry. The restructuring will continue, and securitization will move ahead.

Earlier in this chapter, we noted an important attitude shift in the insurance industry. The result of this shift will eventually establish an important new bridge between the insurance and capital markets. Until recently, there was more talk than action in insurance securitization. Now, however, we are beginning to see multimillion-dollar transactions, such as USAA's $400 million securitization of hurricane risk, the $100 million securitization of Japanese earthquake risk by Parametric Re, and a $280 million deal by Winterthur to securitize the risk of hail damage to automobiles.

Over time, transactions like these will have a snowball effect. We see the same pattern of evolution in other securitized products. Mortgage securitization, for example, started very slowly. It took ten years before a truly viable market existed. Now, however, mortgage-backed securities are commonplace, and the market is highly liquid.

During their lengthy gestation period, securitization markets exhibit a trial-and-error pattern of development. Many products are tested. Eventually, the market responds, and the best products take off. As a consequence, we expect to see many false starts as the industry experiments with insurance securitization ideas. And this experimentation is exactly what we have seen so far.

The Property Claim Services (PCS) catastrophe options contract on the Chicago Board of Trade improved on the original product based on data from the Insurance Services Office. We will see other ideas come along that improve on the PCS catastrophe options. A similar evolution is occurring in the over-the-counter market, with early signs of secondary market trading in recently issued catastrophe-linked instruments.

From a competitive standpoint, securitized products are the expansion team in the insurance league. The reinsurance market is far bigger, quicker, and more fluid. Ultimately, however, there will be a robust insurance securitization market doing all the things being discussed in the other chapters of this book.

As this happens, securitization will have a profound impact on insurance in several dimensions. For one, securitization will lower the cost of risk transfer by attracting new capital and new buyers of insurance risk. The uncorrelated nature of insurance risk relative to the risk of other investments will attract a whole new class of investors seeking to diversify their portfolios. In addition, insurers will be able to reduce the variability in their loss costs by addressing a broader range of underwriting risks through securitization.

Securitization will also change the way insurance companies operate. New ways of analyzing and pricing risks will make it possible for insurers to operate more like investment bankers—focusing on insurance origination and selling the risk off to investors. Processing could also be outsourced, as we have seen with mortgage-backed securities.

Without speculating any further, it's clear that securitization has many exciting implications. Today we see their magnitude. Over the next five to ten years, the details will start to come into focus. For this reason, CNA has decided to participate in securitization now. Insurers who adopt a wait-and-see attitude could find themselves in the same losing position that befell commercial bankers when investment banks began to offer commercial paper as a substitute for loans.

Hedge Financial Products

In early 1997, CNA formed Hedge Financial Products, Inc., to capitalize on opportunities in the emerging business of insurance securitization. With expertise in insurance and capital markets, the staff of Hedge Financial is uniquely suited to bridging the gap between the insurance and capital markets. In fact, several Hedge Financial officers and employees played leading roles in the development of the catastrophe options traded on the Chicago Board of Trade.

Hedge Financial focuses on three areas of opportunity: managing and reducing risk, developing innovative products, and applying technology to the analysis of risk portfolios.

In the area of managing and reducing risk, Hedge Financial is able to tailor solutions to the specific needs of insurance companies and other clients. For example, Hedge Financial and its affiliates can design products that transfer exposures to reinsurers. These exposures, in turn, can be laid off to the capital markets. This risk transfer may be accomplished by developing derivative products to market the embedded exposures to investors or by selling equity or debt instruments linked to the risk.

Hedge Financial may also serve customers by assisting primary underwriters in structuring insurance products with commodity price or financial risk protection features. By working closely with the capital markets, Hedge Financial is able to incorporate nontraditional protection—for exposures such as foreign exchange or interest rate risk—into traditional risk management programs for larger corporate insureds. For example, the insurer of a company dependent on natural gas could provide a combination of property and casualty coverages, along with price protection that insulates the customer from losses stemming from adverse movements in the price of natural gas over a given period. Hedge Financial can then manage the price risk through its expertise in market-based hedging techniques.

Finally, Hedge Financial uses a number of proprietary, state-of-the-art computer models for analyzing and assessing various types of risk. These tools can provide insurance companies with new ways to analyze and optimize the total exposures of their books of insurance business. Since Hedge Financial was formed, much of its work has been with the CNA strategic business units to explore ideas for using securitization techniques. CNA's multiline insurance organization—encompassing 30 different insurance businesses—provides a broad range of opportunities to develop products and transfer risk to the capital markets.

CNA knows that the process may be slow. Hedge Financial will look into a multitude of potential opportunities to find a few that work. CNA views this new venture as a long-term research and development strategy. Ultimately, CNA believes Hedge Financial will become an important business venture and a major competitive advantage for its various insurance and reinsurance businesses.

Future Challenges

Hedge Financial, like every other securitization enterprise, has its own unique strategies and goals. But there are also a set of common challenges. As organizations respond to these challenges, they will shape the evolution of the business.

Basis risk. One of the major issues for insurance securitization is the nature of the risk. Unlike the risks inherent in other securitized products, insurance risk is not homogeneous. Whereas interest rate movements affect all bond prices in the same way, a catastrophe can produce very different loss experiences for identical insurance policies. A windstorm may devastate homes insured by one insurer and only lightly damage the homes insured by another in the same general area. Because of this characteristic, it's difficult to standardize and price a unit of insurance risk.

Over time, however, mechanisms will be developed to solve this problem. As this happens, the insurance securitization market will evolve around a two-tier structure of risk. The first tier will deal with the aggregation of risk and the management of basis risk. Insurance and reinsurance companies operate on this tier now, and they will continue to do so. The second tier will handle the transfer of the aggregated risk to the capital markets. This is the securitization market now in its formative stage.

Investor understanding. Widespread understanding of credit, interest rate, currency, and other risks supports a robust market for securitized financial products. Insurance risk is much less widely understood. As investors gain understanding, they will become more comfortable with securitized insurance products. Until there is a larger pool of knowledgeable counterparties and more opportunities for diversification, however, trading of these products will be limited.

Investors are not alone at the bottom of the learning curve. Securitization also has very different implications for different segments of the insurance industry. We are going to see big differences in the way insurance organizations participate in this new market.

Creating markets. Many indexed insurance derivatives will be developed over the next ten years. Three basic criteria, however, must be satisfied before a robust market will develop around any of them.

First, the index used to value the derivative must relate to some other value determined in a competitive environment. For example, the medical component of the Consumer Price Index might serve as a basis for a derivative used to hedge against changes in health insurance costs. Next, movement of the index must be measurable within a short period of time. The shorter the period, the greater the certainty of the derivative's current price. Finally, the insurance derivative must have a risk-reward relationship that can be duplicated by other investments. This characteristic enables buyers to base their investment decisions on side-by-side comparisons.

Pricing. Despite soft pricing in the reinsurance market, many securitized transactions were oversubscribed in 1997. Pricing has not been a barrier, in spite of the due diligence, marketing, and other transaction frictions inherent in a new class of securities. As buyers and sellers move up the learning curve, these frictional costs will be reduced and the market will continue to grow.

New operating models. As the market for securitized products expands, insurers and reinsurers will manage risk on a daily basis, instead of assuming risk and holding it for the duration of the insurance contract. New operating models will be needed when insurers and reinsurers can fraction the risk in their portfolios and trade in securitized instruments to improve results. Organizations like Hedge Financial will assist insurance organizations in managing the market risks of their trading strategies.

Identifying opportunities. Securitization won't fit in every line of insurance. Catastrophe exposure is the focus of activity so far, but the market will move into other insurance arenas. We will see products that are difficult to imagine today, as well as innovative combinations of insurance, reinsurance, and financial instruments. The emergence of government-sponsored catastrophe programs will affect the nature of these opportunities.

Looking ahead, it's likely that securitization will develop along multiple pathways—many of which are outlined in other chapters of this book. Joint ventures, special purpose reinsurance companies, exchange-traded risk, and customized one-time deals are just a few possibilities.

As the insurance industry advances in these directions, securitization will provide a whole new set of risk financing opportunities. What began as an idea dismissed by much of the insurance industry will emerge as a significant and dynamic component of the financial services infrastructure.

Catastrophe Risk as an "Alternative Investment"

Adam Parkin
The Rangeley Company

According to estimates by InterSec Research, by the end of 1996, investors held US$1 trillion of global assets in "alternative investments," with the growth of this investment sector projected at between 15% and 20% per annum over the next five years. These estimates include increasing investments in catastrophe ("cat") risk.

Defining "alternative investments" provides a clue to the potential appetite for catastrophe risk in the investment community. Alternative investments are generally those that deliver low or negative correlation to the traditional asset classes of cash, bonds, and equities. Such investments include currency, commodities, managed futures, hedge and multi-manager funds, private equity, as well as, in more recent years, catastrophe risk structures.

Catastrophe risk offers an asset class that is not correlated with either the traditional or the existing "alternative" asset classes. Catastrophe risk is, strictly speaking, not a new asset class but one embedded in the fortunes of the reinsurance industry. Yet the performance of insurance industry equities in the United States over the last ten years, relative to the equity market as a whole, does not suggest low or negative correlation. Rather, a comparison of the S&P 500 Index and the S&P Multi-Line Insurers Index (figure 6-1) suggests high correlation.

Figure 6-1 S&P Multi-Line Insurers Index vs. S&P 500 Index, 1988-97

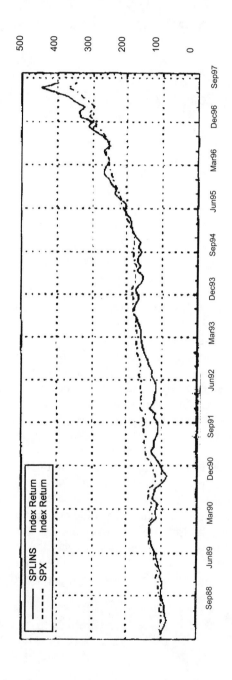

Insurance companies are primarily investment vehicles. Indeed, they are often categorized in the U.K. market as investment trusts with a bad and expensive habit—insurance. While data for the leading U.S. insurers do not bear this out, the fact that their equity is highly correlated with the main share market points to the role of insurance companies as investment holding companies. Even the purest form of catastrophe risk, found in reinsurers, is diluted by the stock and bond assets of these companies.

It is thus difficult—using traditional investments—to separate pure catastrophe risk from the investment risk that the insurance companies have effectively bundled up. Nevertheless, in the modern world of unbundled risks, so facilitated by the derivatives markets, investors want to create their own portfolios of transparent risk. The Chicago Board of Trade (CBOT) catastrophe insurance options and other forms of securitized catastrophe risk are means by which investors can arrange their own levels of risk within their asset portfolios.

Cat Risk in a Portfolio

As with most alternative investments, the addition of cat risk should improve the efficiency of a standard portfolio. The portfolio benefits not only from the high expected returns, but also from the noncorrelation inherent in cat risk.

That's because catastrophe losses tend not to follow any recognizable pattern, least of all the smooth lognormal pattern of returns beloved of the financial markets. Not only do catastrophes tend to occur infrequently and with variable severity, but the underlying probability distribution is largely a mystery. This feature of cat risk explains the apparent supranormal returns. It is only over the very long run that investors might be confident about a discernible risk distribution and whether prices could be deemed "fair value."

Figure 6-2 illustrates the virtues of cat risk within a diversified global portfolio of risk, using Swiss Re simulations of cat risk based on Property Claim Services (PCS) U.S. catastrophe data. Whether for a U.S.-only or for a global stock and bond portfolio, the addition of cat risk improves the efficiency of the portfolio, producing more return per unit of risk.

The optimal amount of cat risk in any portfolio depends upon the risk and return preferences of individual investors. As figure 6-3 shows, the higher the target return, the larger the desired amount of cat risk in the portfolio. Indeed, the further out one moves on the risk or volatility spectrum, the more the low risk and return assets, such as short-term bonds, are replaced by catastrophe risk.

Figure 6-2 Efficient Portfolios: Adding Cat Risk

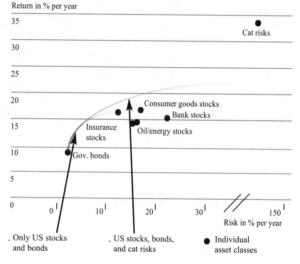

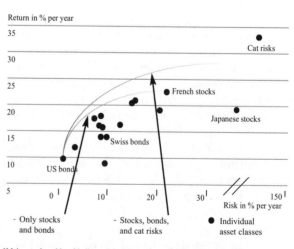

Figure 6-3 Efficient Portfolios: Increasing Cat Risk

Portfolio return: 10% per year
Portfolio risk: 1.4% per year

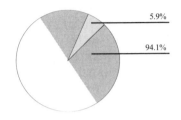

5.9%

94.1%

Portfolio return: 12% per year
Portfolio risk: 1.75% per year

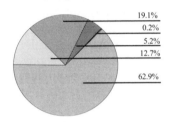

19.1%
0.2%
5.2%
12.7%
62.9%

Portfolio return: 14% per year
Portfolio risk: 2.5% per year

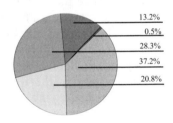

13.2%
0.5%
28.3%
37.2%
20.8%

Portfolio return: 16% per year
Portfolio risk: 3.6% per year

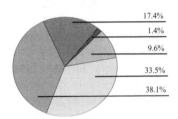

17.4%
1.4%
9.6%
33.5%
38.1%

Portfolio return: 18% per year
Portfolio risk: 5.0% per year

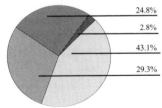

24.8%
2.8%
43.1%
29.3%

Portfolio return: 20% per year
Portfolio risk: 7.5% per year

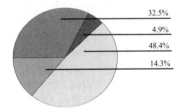

32.5%
4.9%
48.4%
14.3%

- ■ US cat risks
- ■ Asian assets
- ▨ European assets
- ▨ US stocks
- ▨ US bonds

Source: Swiss Re

The reverse applies to the portfolios of the Lloyd's market. The "names," or investors, in Lloyd's have traditionally underwritten a variety of insurance risks backed by the most conservative of investments, typically short-dated U.S. and U.K. government bonds. With the annual account structure and the leverage inherent in underwriting insurance risk, there has been a reluctance to expand the investment scope in the London market. Yet the addition of global bonds, stocks, or other alternative investments, provided high standards of liquidity are maintained, should be more efficient than the very traditional Lloyd's portfolios.

Warren Buffett's Secret Weapon

Diversification and the improved efficiency of a portfolio in terms of high return and minimized variance is the classical paradigm. As in many areas of human activity, it takes a master to challange the orthodox. In investment, Warren Buffett is an acknowledged master. Rather than diversify, he prefers to concentrate on a limited number of primarily U.S. stocks. Even so, his portfolio includes a significant exposure to insurance, particularly cat risk. Indeed, according to Standard & Poor's, Berkshire Hathaway was the 20th largest consolidated reinsurer in the world in 1995, with $781 million net premium written and practically no retrocessions.

Berkshire Hathaway's insurance operations began in March 1967 with the purchase of National Indemnity Company and National Fire & Marine Insurance Company. Berkshire continued to expand aggressively in the early 1970s, buying a number of insurance businesses, a policy that persisted until conditions deteriorated sharply with overcapacity in the insurance market. Unlike the typical insurance company, Buffett's Berkshire has not been tempted to write large volumes of premium at soft rates for the sake of maintaining market share.

Indeed, the major acquisition of GEICO Corporation (Government Employees Insurance Company) took place in 1976 after GEICO fell afoul of overexpansionary policies. By 1980, GEICO had become the largest holding in the Berkshire portfolio. Buffett restored GEICO to its pre-1970s roots, a strategy that successfully returned the company to earning an underwriting profit on the insurance policies it issued. Most important, GEICO managed its investment portfolio with exceptional results. From 1979 to 1989, the company's equity portfolio grew at 26.1% a year (S&P 500 17.4%); from 1990 to 1993, it grew at 16.5% a year (S&P 500 10.8%). The business has been so successful that Berkshire acquired complete control of GEICO in early 1996, paying $2.3 billion for the remaining 49% of the business. Being a low-cost operator and profitable underwriter remain the competitive strengths of the company.

Berkshire has continued its policy of buying attractive insurance operations. In 1996, Buffet acquired the Kansas Banker's Surety, another company with an exceptional underwriting record. Berkshire has more recently participated in the super-catastrophe insurance business, covering primarily Florida hurricane and California earthquake risk.

Berkshire's business consists of two distinct elements: the insurance business and the core investment business. Insurance, whether primary or super-catastrophe, feeds the investments of the company. Buffett himself acknowledges the importance of the amount of the "float," and its price, provided by the insurance business. The "float" (plus deferred tax liabilities) constitutes Berkshire's "borrowed" money and effectively gives Buffett leverage in his investments.

The "float" from an insurance business is the money accumulated from premiums received before losses are paid. If losses exceed premiums, the company suffers an underwriting loss. If premiums exceed losses, the company's underwriting profits. Given the lumpy nature of cat risk, it is possible only over the longer run to judge whether a company is accumulating profits or losses from its insurance activities. Yet as table 6-1 shows, Buffett's insurance activities have tended to be profitable.

Table 6-1 Berkshire Hathaway: Volume and Price of the Berkshire "Float"

	(1) Underwriting Loss	(2) Average Float*	(3) Approximate Cost of Funds** Ratio of (1) to (2) (% per year)	(4) Year-end Yield on Long-term Government Bonds
	(in $ millions)			
1967	profit	17.3	less than zero	5.50%
1968	profit	19.9	less than zero	5.90%
1969	profit	23.4	less than zero	6.79%
1970	0.37	32.4	1.14%	6.25%
1971	profit	52.5	less than zero	5.81%
1972	profit	69.5	less than zero	5.82%
1973	profit	73.3	less than zero	7.27%
1974	7.36	79.1	9.30%	8.13%

Table 6-1 Berkshire Hathaway: Volume and Price of the Berkshire "Float," *con't.*

	(1) Underwriting Loss	(2) Average Float*	(3) Approximate Cost of Funds** Ratio of (1) to (2) (% per year)	(4) Year-end Yield on Long-term Government Bonds
		(in $ millions)		
1975	11.35	87.6	12.96%	8.03%
1976	profit	102.6	less than zero	7.30%
1977	profit	139.0	less than zero	7.97%
1978	profit	190.4	less than zero	8.93%
1979	profit	227.3	less than zero	10.08%
1980	profit	237.0	less than zero	11.94%
1981	profit	228.4	less than zero	13.61%
1982	21.56	220.6	9.77%	10.64%
1983	33.87	231.3	14.64%	11.84%
1984	48.06	253.2	18.98%	11.58%
1985	44.23	390.2	11.34%	9.34%
1986	55.84	797.5	7.00%	7.60%
1987	55.43	1266.7	4.38%	8.95%
1988	11.08	1497.7	0.74%	9.00%
1989	24.40	1541.3	1.58%	7.97%
1990	26.65	1637.3	1.63%	8.24%
1991	119.59	1895.0	6.31%	7.40%
1992	108.96	2290.4	4.76%	7.39%
1993	profit	2624.7	less than zero	6.35%
1994	profit	3056.6	less than zero	7.88%
1995	profit	3607.2	less than zero	5.95%
1996	profit	6702.0	less than zero	6.64%

*The float is calculated by adding loss reserves, loss adjustment reserves, funds held under reinsurance assumed, and unearned premium reserves, and then subtracting agents' balances, prepared acquisition costs, prepaid taxes, and deferred charges applicable to assumed reinsurance.

**The cost of the float is the underwriting loss or profit. When there is an underwriting profit, the cost of float is negative, and Berkshire is paid to borrow.

Source: Berkshire Hathaway Annual Report 1996

The data from table 6-1 show that over the past 30 years, Berkshire incurred a significant loss in only five years: 1974-75 and 1983-85, when the approximate cost of funds exceeded the year-end yield on long-term government bonds. In every other year, Berkshire either earned a profit from its underwriting activities or incurred a small loss, which, expressed as a cost to the company, was less than the market rate for funds. Buffett prefers to use a long-term bond yield rather than a short-term bank loan rate as the appropriate benchmark. In using insurance underwriting as a means of achieving "leverage," Berkshire over time has substantially improved its financing terms in comparison with borrowing in the bank or bond markets.

While Berkshire has demonstrated considerable success over time, any insurance business must be very aware of the potential losses from the insurance portfolio. In particular, the super-catastrophe business could frighten many investors. Buffett stresses that the excellent results from Berkshire in recent years are in part due to the super-cat business having a "lucky" year. Unlike more conventional insurance, the super-cat business has a very "lumpy" profile, earning high profits in many years with an occasional large loss. In Buffett's words, "What you must understand, however, is that a truly terrible year in the super-cat business is not a possibility—it's a certainty. The only question is when it will come."

Berkshire's involvement in the super-catastrophe business stems from the large catastrophes incurred in North America from 1992 to 1994. These events prompted California, Florida, and Hawaii to create catastrophe funds to act as reinsurers of last resort. Insurers underwriting risk in these states can buy protection from these funds for their extreme exposures.

In the case of California, the California Earthquake Authority initially looked for the bulk of its funding from the state's own property insurance market. Furthermore, the CEA intended to raise $1.5 billion through "catastrophe bonds" sold to institutional investors. As it happened, however, Berkshire provided the cover at a premium of 10%, as opposed to a premium of 14.5% envisaged in the original deal. The Berkshire/CEA deal, while fixed for March 1996, will continue to March 2001, with premiums estimated at $590 million. The deductible on the deal is $7 billion in insured losses. In its 1996 annual report, Berkshire estimated its likely maximum loss at $600 million, which suggests that even in the event of underwriting losses, deemed a low probability, the company has secured a large volume of funds to add to its float.

Note, too, the "fixed rate" reinsurance implied by the terms of the deal, struck to March 2001. More traditional reinsurance—replicated by the structure of the CBOT derivatives—involves striking annual "floating rate" deals. Clearly the judgment as to whether "fixed" or "floating" rein- surance is more profitable depends on the position in the underwriting cycle and the likely progress of rates on line. If rates on line are expect- ed to harden or rise, then an underwriter of risk should prefer floating deals. For the investor, the choice of fixed or floating deals is one of fine- tuning, given the decision already made to add cat risk to the portfolio.

Diversifying the Portfolio

Cat risk, by its nature, should be constructed within a highly diversified portfolio. Insurance is typically managed on a law of large numbers basis, that is, many risks where the consequences of an individual loss are small. Unfortunately, property catastrophe risk, in a manageable and reasonably liquid form, is still largely confined to the North American market. Despite quite different loss experiences for West Coast earthquake and East Coast hurricane exposures, insufficient diversification possibilities remain a problem.

The following example illustrates the problem. The example takes a spread of North American risk and simulates portfolio underwriting results over a 10-year period to the end of 1995, based on premium rates at the end of 1996 and actual PCS data over the period for the respective risks. The portfolio attempts a spread of working layers of risk, typically the most frequently traded PCS index layers on the CBOT, which reflect the actual loss experience. Tables 6-2 and 6-3 summarize the portfolio and the underwriting results.

As table 6-2 shows, US$7 million out of a total US$29.15 million, or 24% of total premium, is written on the National annual contract for the 100/120 layer, with US$20 million at risk of loss. In both 1992 and 1994, this contract would have resulted in a full loss, leaving a deficit of US$13 million in each year.

Table 6-3 shows the negative underwriting results spread across the spectrum. In 1992 and 1994, losses were substantial and would be hard to bear for many investors, particularly those starting to invest in cat risk at that time. If underwriting had started in 1986 and good investment acquired, then a substantial reserve would have been accrued by 1992. An attractive underwriting profit of $63.19 million would have been made over the whole period, on written premium annually of $29.15 million. This underwriting profit makes no allowance for the investment returns earned on the accumulated premiums.

Table 6-2 A Sample Portfolio of CBOT Catastrophe Risk (late 1996-early 1997) (spread of most frequently traded contracts)

	Contract		Layer	Premium $m	Amount at Risk $m	Rate on Line
1	National	Annual	100/120	7	20	35%
2	Southeast	Sep	60/80	3	20	15%
3	Texas	Jun/Sep/Dec	5/30	5.5	25	22%
4	Midwest	June	10/20	1.5	10	15%
5	Northeast	Sep	40/60	1.8	20	9%
6	Eastern	Sep/Dec	40/60	4.5	20	22½%
7	Western	Annual	80/100	2.1	20	10½%
8	National	March	20/40	3.75	20	18¾%
			Total	**29.15**	**155**	**18.8%**

Sources: CBOT, Hedge Financial Products

Table 6-3 Simulated Underwriting Results, 1986-95
Spread of North American Contracts (see table 6-2)
[assuming the same premium is written each year of the ten years]

$m	1	2	3	4	5	6	7	8	Total
1986	7	3	5½	1½	1.8	4½	2.1	3¾	29.15
1987	7	3	5½	1½	1.8	4½	2.1	3¾	29.15
1988	7	3	5½	1½	1.8	4½	2.1	3¾	29.15
1989	7	3	0.6	1½	1.8	-15½	2.1	3¾	4.25
1990	7	3	5½	1½	1.8	4½	2.1	3¾	29.15
1991	7	3	2.9	1½	1.8	4½	2.1	3¾	26.55
1992	-13	-17	-2.6	-3.6	1.8	-15½	2.1	3¾	-44.05
1993	7	3	5½	1½	1.8	4½	2.1	-3.55	21.85
1994	-13	3	2.6	1½	1.8	4½	-17.9	-16.25	-33.75
1996	7	3	-9.8	1½	1.8	4½	2.1	3¾	13.95
Loss Ratio (%)	57.1	66.7	61.5	34.0	0	88.9	95.2	72.8	63.9

Sources: CBOT, Hedge Financial Products

If the portfolio were more diversified, including non-North American risk for example, then the stream of returns from underwriting would likely be less lumpy, more continuous, and more familiar to most investors. A more diversified portfolio is characteristic of the larger global reinsurance companies. The recent drive for consolidation in the industry in part reflects this need for diversification.

The Scope for Development

While cat risk clearly has appeal, not least in a theoretical sense, the small scale of the asset globally points to relative illiquidity. It is estimated that the capital and surplus in the U.S. market for primary insurers and reinsurers is approximately $225 billion, in comparison with the $120 trillion in the U.S. capital markets. With a daily standard deviation of roughly $140 billion, the capital markets have a huge capacity for underwriting risk. Structuring cat risks in a manner familiar to those in interest rate, currency, and equity markets, whether through "securitization" in cat bonds or through derivatives in CBOT-type contracts, increases the likelihood of more rapid integration in the capital markets.

The CBOT approach has considerable appeal. The CBOT market allows investors to underwrite risk based on past statistical experience and standardized contracts. The absence of moral hazard, adverse selection, or problems with a particular cedent should encourage investors. For hedgers, however, more used to traditional insurance risks, there is the problem of basis risk between insurance risk at the micro level and the standardized contracts on the CBOT. This problem of cat basis risk, as it appears today, is possibly less tractable than with the more traditional financial asset markets. If hedgers remain reluctant to tackle basis risk, an important source of liquidity will be missing.

Inevitably, liquidity is all-important for many investors. But in the life cycle of the development of a market or product, returns are likely to be higher the more illiquid the market. Indeed, the pioneers having to bear the high risks should enjoy the more lucrative returns.

Cat risk will undoubtedly appear in portfolios in a variety of ways. The Warren Buffett method seems a sensible starting point. Cat risk is managed within Berkshire in a similar manner to a currency overlay program. An investor's existing portfolio can function as collateral for the potential insurance liabilities, with cedents needing to assess the strength of the collateral in relation to the mix of liabilities acquired. In particular, the way is open for the ubiquitous hedge fund or fund of funds to combine with cat risk and expand the frontier of investment possibilities.

Chapter 7

Reinsurance Brokers Redefined

Frank Majors
Greg Hagood
Willis Corroon Catastrophe Management

Redefining the role of reinsurance brokers in this period of reinsurance and capital market "convergence" isn't easy. Yet that's exactly what reinsurance brokers must do as they react to the new threats and opportunities and attempt to leverage their existing strengths.

The roles that brokers are choosing to play are almost as numerous as the broking houses. In its innovative response to securitization, Willis Faber Re, the reinsurance broking subsidiary of Willis Corroon Group, formed Willis Corroon Catastrophe Management (WCCM), a fund for institutional investors dedicated to the emerging insurance securitization asset class. But this initiative is just one of several strategies being employed by brokers.

This chapter attempts to explain how the role of the reinsurance broker is evolving and why that role is being defined in such a varied way by industry participants. Willis Faber Re's strategy, like those of its competitors, says a lot about the particular expertise it has and will attempt to leverage in carving out a role in this developing market. We will examine the following factors to determine why members of the broking community have taken such varied approaches:

- the broker's traditional functions, both primary and secondary
- the situation facing brokers, which serves as a backdrop for strategy formulation
- strengths and weaknesses of the broking community
- varied strategies, including an overview of Willis Faber Re's WCCM initiative

Note that a lot has been written in recent years about the convergence of the capital and reinsurance markets, with talk of lines blurring between the two. The following is based on the view that this "convergence" of two markets is actually the "development" of one: the continued evolution of a distinct and clearly defined "reinsurance capital market." The focus of this chapter is on the specific role that brokers will play in the evolving reinsurance capital market. It does not fully address the role that brokers will continue to play in traditional reinsurance.

Traditional Functions

The past few years have seen incredible change in the insurance and reinsurance industry. Perhaps no participant in this arena has been forced to examine and reevaluate its position more than the reinsurance broker. Fortunately, most brokers tend to be resilient and innovative, accustomed to adapting to market shocks.

In past times of turmoil, the reinsurance broker's role was clear: help clients determine their exposures, structure programs and develop products to protect those exposures, and distribute those exposures to reinsurance companies. Brokers understood that other services, such as claims handling and contract preparation, were part of account maintenance. The broker's traditional view of its role could be expressed by a very simple diagram (see figure 7-1).

The changes currently taking place, however, have been particularly challenging, since they are forcing each of the major reinsurance brokers to define exactly what role it will play, and which of the several skill sets and areas of expertise it will leverage, in the convergent reinsurance capital market. To understand the choices faced by brokers, one must understand their traditional roles—roles which still, by and large, exist. The fact that a broker is traditionally hired by the insurance company but is paid by the reinsurer points to the dilemma confronting the broker. It is a consultant to the insurance company (the client) but is the distribution system of reinsurers.

Figure 7-1 Reinsurance Brokers' Traditional Role—Simplified

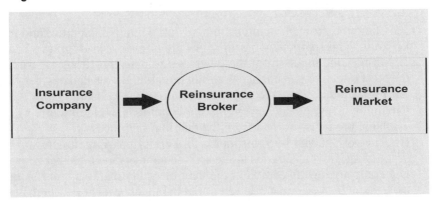

The services provided by reinsurance brokers can be divided into primary (functional services of direct benefit to the client) and secondary (more subtle benefits which accrue to the market as a whole and which form the basis of expertise used in providing primary services). As insurance companies gradually sought more service from brokers, each of the functions had to be defined and augmented. The three primary functions can be broken down as follows.

Consulting on Technical Issues

Only in recent years have the major reinsurance brokers raised this function to a science. Catastrophe exposures are now quantified using complex computer simulations rather than intuition or rules of thumb. For example, Willis Faber Re has formed a research & development team that combines actuaries, geographers, and computer modelers to build complex geophysical models of the world's natural hazards. This R&D team models each client's portfolio so that the resulting loss forecasts reflect the client's underwriting and policy profiles.

Information derived from this process is a valuable input for brokers when structuring a program or designing a product for an insurance company. Also, by combining catastrophe modeling with advanced actuarial models, brokers can consider the probabilities of losses and their return periods and therefore evaluate the price of risk. This type of scientific analysis allows the broking organization to perform an invaluable function with increased precision, replacing the former and less reliable guideline of intuition.

Structuring Programs and Designing Products

This function probably requires the greatest degree of expertise and market knowledge, particularly with respect to pricing risk. It forces a broker to consider the inputs from the other two primary functions to structure the most effective reinsurance program possible. It's a balancing act, with the broker addressing the risks identified in the consulting role while remaining aware of the current market conditions, including pricing and available products, learned from the distribution process.

The role played by reinsurance brokers in program structuring and product design is analogous to the service an investment banker provides to a company raising capital in the debt or equity markets. For example, investment bankers must price an initial public offering at a level that will achieve the company's goals, yet they must also base that level on prevailing market conditions.

Marketing and Distributing the Programs/Products

Of the three primary functions, perhaps the marketing function most clearly represents the traditional view of the reinsurance broker, as it is the most visible role played. This step in the process is critical—the point at which deals are actually struck. It is most analogous to institutional sales and is dependent both upon a detailed knowledge of the program and upon strong market relationships.

Figure 7-2 diagrams the consulting-structuring-distribution view of the reinsurance broker. Recent events notwithstanding, reinsurance brokers have traditionally functioned in this fashion.

The Broker's Environment

Against this background, consider some of the "agents of change" forcing reinsurance brokers to redefine themselves even further. Consolidation in the industry means fewer companies actually buying reinsurance, fewer reinsurers for the ceding insurance company to know (thereby diminishing part of the value clients historically counted on brokers to provide, a sort of "roster of players"), and stronger companies less dependent upon the reinsurance market as a source of capital. In addition, as brokers continue to consolidate, each broker finds itself in an "arms race" of added services that are often difficult to price, especially in the traditional bundled services approach.

Figure 7-2 Reinsurance Brokers' Traditional Role—Augmented

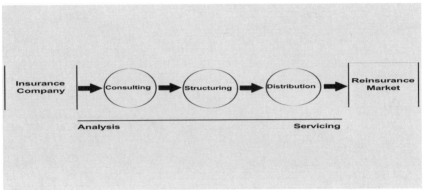

Other factors are at work as well. The long bull markets in bonds and equities have certainly increased general knowledge of and comfort with capital markets, and many companies in the insurance industry have participated in recent years with share offerings and through mergers or acquisitions. These developments make for a more sophisticated reinsurance broker client, a client more aware than ever of the opportunities available and who has strong relationships with investment bankers and the analysts who follow the company. These factors have contributed to a subtle change in the client's perception of risk and of ways to manage it, and brokers have been forced to keep up with the learning curve.

Brokers also face competition from new entrants, such as investment banks. Here the reinsurance broker must realize that each new entrant is competing with the broker on different fronts by clearly defining which function it will perform. While existing brokers have attempted to offer more and more services, often bundled as one "product," their new competitors are emphasizing their particular skills and expertise.

For example, competition arises from dedicated exposure modelers offering analytical services to insurance companies, helping them determine portfolio exposures without providing the additional services of program structuring and risk distribution. Some brokers planning to provide licensed industry information now find themselves in competition with firms never considered as adversaries, such as the Insurance Services Office (ISO) and Property Claim Services (PCS), two long-standing organizations created specifically as clearinghouses for insurance industry information. Investment bankers, for their part, are arguing that reinsurance is simply another form of capital and therefore part of the insurance company's capital structure. The natural extension of this logic is for the bankers to offer their services in structuring financial products and distributing those products to investors.

With these new developments, reinsurance brokers have been forced to view themselves and their environment along the more intricate lines diagrammed in figure 7-3. It's been interesting to observe diverse reactions to this altered playing field. The strategy (or strategies) implemented by each of the broking houses could be seen as that company's answer to the question posed at the beginning of this analysis: What is the role of the reinsurance broker in this new market structure? Because of the wide array of services traditionally provided by brokers, it is unlikely that many companies would choose the same response. Rather, each company will choose a strategy that highlights those aspects of the traditional broking process which it believes it can leverage in the developing reinsurance capital market.

Figure 7-3 Reinsurance Brokers in the New Market Structure

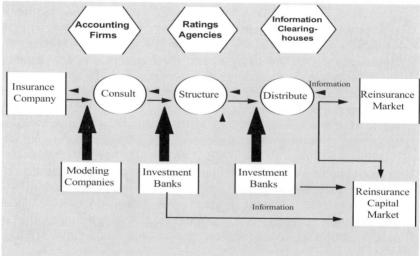

The Broking Community's Strengths and Weaknesses

Before examining a few of the strategies that the major reinsurance brokers have implemented, we should identify some of unique expertise and resources developed in the reinsurance broking industry over the years:

Strengths	Weaknesses
- Risk pricing	- Lack strong distribution to investors
- Historical data	- Lack strong balance sheets
- Relationships with insurance companies (including knowledge of exposures and cultures and expectations with respect to account service)	
- Understanding of reinsurance companies (including pricing parameters and constraints)	
- Experience (at individual and institutional levels)	

These valuable assets have not developed in a matter of a few years or even a few decades. Brokers have an incredible amount of data built up from the business process over many years. For example, a study of Hurricane Andrew conducted recently by Willis Faber Re required analysis of over 270,000 data entries from one business unit alone. Another important asset that positions the broker well in the developing reinsurance capital market is the trading mentality found in many of the broking houses. This approach to risk as a tradeable commodity, combined with the massive databases derived from handling a wide base of business, gives reinsurance brokers an impressive advantage in pricing and understanding securitized insurance risk.

Experience is probably the most difficult asset to quantify. The financial press is fond of questioning how investment managers who have seen only bull markets will respond to a bear market or stock market crash. The same question can be asked of capital market players now adding securitized risk to their investment portfolios. If a major catastrophe happens (e.g., $30 billion hurricane), how will investors' insurance portfolios respond? How will the investors themselves respond to losing principal? In such circumstances, the experience that reinsurance brokers have in anticipating and surviving tough markets will be invaluable.

Varied Strategies

With such a broad set of skills from which to choose, members of the broking community have reacted with a variety of approaches. The following outline divides the responses into four main groups: structuring and distribution, product development, information provider, and investment management. Note that the strategies are in no way mutually exclusive and that several companies, including Willis Faber Re, are adopting more than one approach.

The following does suggest that, at least in the context of the converging markets, reinsurance brokers are unbundling the traditional services and selling their expertise piecemeal to different participants, depending upon the particular need of the client. The result is that the broker no longer just counts insurance companies as clients, but can add investors, bond issuers, and investment banks to the list as well.

Deal Structurer/Distributor

Not surprisingly, the initial primary response of the reinsurance broking houses to convergence was to view capital market developments as a threat. They originally saw no alternative other than fighting to maintain their most visible historical role as the distributor of risk transfer products and therefore began to offer broker/dealer services to their insurance company clients. In doing so, they became direct competitors of the investment banking community.

Intuitively, this response was based on the belief that regardless of which market ultimately accepts the risk, and regardless of which product transfers that risk (reinsurance contract/insurance-linked derivative/catastrophe bond), the relevant feature of the product is the underlying risk—an understanding of which reinsurance brokers possess. Reinsurance brokers simply needed greater skills with respect to the new products to provide full structuring and distribution to their traditional client base. As a result of this view, broking houses began developing or buying broker/dealer capabilities, including registering for appropriate securities licenses.

In the past several years, broking houses have progressed a great deal on the structuring side. Companies soon found, however, that the ability to put together a deal is of limited value without the ability to distribute that deal to investors. Unfortunately, reinsurance brokers' distribution to investors is still virtually nonexistent when compared to the huge distribution networks of the major investment banks. Just as investment banks found that the skills possessed by reinsurance brokers are not acquired overnight, reinsurance brokers found that product distribution is not easily developed.

Who wins this battle, of course, depends on how insurance company clients view the new market—and on what skills they seek in an intermediary. The early results tend to support the investment banks, as the majority of deals have been completed with investment bankers acting as intermediaries. This early success could be attributed to a curiosity/innovation factor on behalf of the issuing companies. Alternatively, it could mean that when choosing an institution to structure and distribute risk to the developing market, understanding the underlying risk is less important than structuring and, especially, distribution.

Product Development

Some brokers have attempted to build "brand identity" for certain types of transactions that address specific needs or unique situations. These products can generally be classified as hybrids of capital market and reinsurance transactions, often using either reinsurance structures or capital or both. What differentiates these deals is that the objectives are usually associated with the capital markets (e.g., equity financing or leveraging capital).

For example, a few reinsurance brokers in the London market, including Willis Faber Re, have succeeded in placing "gearing" arrangements for Lloyd's corporate capital vehicles. These arrangements address a particular need of certain market players. Specifically, they allow corporate investors in Lloyd's syndicates to increase the level of premium written for a given level of capital—basically, a type of margin account for underwriting. Another example is the successful placement by Aon of its contingent equity product, CatEPuts. These products allow a company to negotiate the price at which it can raise capital in the future in the event of certain losses. Development of these products represents a strategy most closely aligned with the traditional role of the reinsurance broker, since it encompasses the full range of services brokers can provide, including product innovation.

"Third Party" Information Provider

New entrants to the market have forced reinsurance brokers to examine what resources they have that are not available to the new competitors. Many have found that they have access to an incredible amount of valuable data. Going beyond the value that historical data provides as an input for analysis, a few brokers have decided that they are in the best position to be information providers for participants in the new reinsurance capital market.

Two examples are Sedgwick's Instrat and Guy Carpenter's IndexCo. These companies are developing indices which they hope will be adopted as benchmarks by investors and insurance companies and which will therefore find use in securities or derivatives linked to such benchmark indices. Revenues come in the form of a licensing fee paid by parties wishing to use a particular index. This strategy leverages the traditional reinsurance broker's consulting skills and information advantage.

"Securitized" Investment Management

Securitization is based on the concept of insurance companies accessing capital directly rather than through the reinsurance market. The benefits are assumed to be transactional efficiencies and access to a far greater pool of capital. Yet the nature of insurance risk is very different from the risks that institutional investors are used to analyzing and managing and therefore requires special expertise to be incorporated profitably into a portfolio.

We believe that securitized insurance risk offers a very attractive asset class to institutional investors, but we recognize the hurdles that prevent some from participating. Specifically, most investors lack experience and dedicated resources to price and manage insurance risk, thereby making the risk of adverse selection very real. If a professional insurance company is offering insurance risk through an intermediary serving as its agent, how do uninformed investors know whether they are being properly compensated for the risk taken? Prospectuses so far have done an impressive job of trying to address this concern, but the doubts surely linger. And once an instrument is added to a portfolio, how do the investors monitor their performance and prevent an accumulation of exposures?

Willis Corroon Catastrophe Management is based on the premise that reinsurance brokers in general, and Willis Faber Re in particular, have access to valuable information and have developed expertise over the years which is valuable to institutional investors. Willis Faber Re considered several alternative ways to sell this expertise, including rating catastrophe bonds and consulting to individual investors. Ultimately, we decided that the most comprehensive and effective approach to incorporating the full range of our in-house expertise came in the form of a managed fund dedicated solely to securitized insurance risk and run by full-time managers with access to Willis Faber Re's resources.

By allocating capital to the Willis Corroon Catastrophe Investment Fund, investors can add this developing asset class to their portfolio while overcoming the management problems inherent in this unique risk. The fund is run by two full-time managers (with oversight by a dedicated compliance officer) who have access to reinsurance actuaries, a proprietary catastrophe options pricing model, historical insurance industry data, and access to the traditional reinsurance brokers for help in analysis, among other valuable resources.

This strategy is based on the belief that the unique expertise reinsurance brokers have is a knowledge of the underlying risk, rather than packaging and distributing that risk. Even more, at this stage of development, we believe that it is the one piece of the puzzle not being provided. In our view, the fund should remove the final hurdle for investors, leading to an influx of capital to propel development of this "emerging" market.

The fund was launched at the beginning of April 1998, with a variety of institutional investors participating: life insurance companies, hedge funds, tax-exempt endowments, and foundations and captives. The fund is currently closed to new investors, though the managers plan to offer additional subscriptions in early 1999, subject to continued market growth.

The continued development of the reinsurance capital market has presented a threat and an opportunity to reinsurance brokers. As they have done during past periods of dramatic change, the major broking houses have responded with innovation and creativity. Willis Faber Re is pleased with the response that the Willis Corroon Catastrophe Investment Fund has received from the institutional investment community. Nonetheless, we will continue to develop strategies to exploit changes in the marketplace, and we are certain that our competitors will do the same.

The Role of Computer Modeling in Insurance Risk Securitization

Tom Hutton
Risk Management Solutions, Inc.

Early transactions transferring or financing catastrophe risk from insurers and reinsurers to capital markets investors have demonstrated a far more central role for third-party risk modeling and simulation than expected. While investment banks and other financial intermediaries had broadly anticipated a process that would emphasize the issuer's reputation for underwriting quality, there is now evidence that risk modeling is of equal importance to key constituents, particularly rating agencies and investors.

Modeling catastrophe risk provides a relevant measure for all constituents that is otherwise unavailable because of the low frequency of events (very few historical data points) and the changing nature of the exposures (historical data points do not represent consistent structures, values, or portfolios). The role of modeling has been similar in both rated and nonrated transactions. For nonrated transactions, the role of modeling is similar to the role of ratings in rated transactions: it provides an independent perspective and benchmark. For rated transactions, the rating agencies have validated the approach and effectiveness of the models provided by commercial vendors, with the resulting security rating reflecting both the modeled probabilities of various expected returns and the quality and dependability of the data, the model, and the analysis process.

This chapter discusses the current and expected role of modeling in the securitization of insurance and reinsurance risk transfer (based on the catastrophe risk example). It specifically addresses:

- the current role of modeling
- what modeling is done, and why it has become so important
- analogies from other markets and lessons learned from early transactions
- the current formula for success
- expected developments in the use of models in risk securitization

The Current Role of Modeling

As an example of the current role of modeling, consider the case history of RMS's typical engagement in a securities offering. The process goes through seven phases.

Phase 1: Feasibility analysis. A prospective issuer or its intermediary approaches the modeling analyst with a potential transaction. Feasibility analysis includes a review and potential enhancement of available exposure data and a preliminary risk modeling analysis to determine how key loss statistics compare with standards developed from recent transactions. The securitization is considered feasible if the data quality is acceptable and if the resulting risk/loss modeling suggests that the required security yield will compare favorably with alternatives. These alternatives include risk retention by the prospective issuer, risk mitigation through internal portfolio management mechanisms, and traditional reinsurance risk transfer.

The prospective issuer may consider a structure that is based on an index or that otherwise results in some retention of *basis risk* (the difference between the risk transferred and the actual underlying risk to the insurer or reinsurer). In this case, the feasibility analysis would include an assessment of the level of basis risk, the options for minimizing or transferring this risk, and the acceptability of the outcome for the prospective issuer. The duration of the feasibility analysis process is a function of how efficiently the various parties work together, which clearly happens best in an ongoing service relationship. Typically, feasibility analyses require two to three weeks' time.

Phase 2: Portfolio analysis (baseline risk and loss analysis). The entire securitization, including final security structuring, rating, and pricing, will be based on a modeled loss analysis. This analysis outputs the expected losses for specific events and situations, expected average losses over the duration of the issue, and the uncertainty factors used for risk loading in computing expected price and yield profiles. The time required for baseline analysis is largely a function of whether the modeling analyst has prior experience with the portfolio. It can take between two and four weeks.

Phase 3: Security structuring. While the actual structure is typically defined by the issuer and its investment banking advisor, the modeling analyst is actively involved in the process. The role of modeling is to optimize the effectiveness of the structure for the issuer (minimal basis risk, maximum effective risk transfer as a function of expected cost). Typically, the modeling analyst works closely with other advisors to accomplish these structuring goals. This phase is not always sequential and can take as little as one day or as long as several weeks.

Phase 4: Rating agency review. The rating agencies will each review the modeling methodologies, the implementation (software), and its application in the specific analysis. To the extent that the rating agencies have worked with the model before, this process is far quicker and far more certain. The rating agencies will each review and test several assumptions and outputs of the specific analysis. These tests are currently different at each rating agency. This phase can take from two to five weeks.

Phase 5: Offering prospectus and disclosure documentation. The offering prospectus contains a substantial amount of information about the model, the modeling approach, and the specific analysis performed as part of the securitization (phase 2). Early transactions have required considerable time for documentation, because the investment bankers, modeling analysts, and attorneys are typically developing such documentation for the first time. The time required to develop the documentation depends on the complexity of the transaction and the prior experience of the advisors.

Phase 6: Investor interface. Each of the major investor marketing meetings, including both private meetings and the group "road show" presentations, focus considerable attention on modeling. Presentations are thorough, and any conceivable questions about the modeling are addressed. There is absolutely no room for nondisclosure of assumptions or "black box" mystery of methods. If an approach cannot be defended or defined, it should not be used. Recent transactions have been fully subscribed within the first two to three weeks of marketing.

Phase 7: Ongoing responsibilities. The modeling analyst often retains ongoing responsibilities for the duration of the security, which in some cases have included remodeling the portfolio following its growth or following individual events. For example, one recent transaction (Trinity Re) employed a reset mechanism whereby the portfolio is reanalyzed following any potentially triggering event to remove the uncertainty risk of portfolio growth from the investor.

In total, a securitization of catastrophe risk currently requires approximately eight to twelve weeks from conception to completion. Overall, the time requirements are dramatically reduced if the prospective issuer has maintained a regular modeled analysis of its portfolio risk, effectively avoiding phases 1 and 2 and making the remaining phases far more efficient.

Risk Modeling and Securitization

Over the past five to ten years, property insurers and reinsurers have increasingly relied on sophisticated computer simulation models to quantify potential losses and overall risk from natural catastrophes. By far the most widely used are the models provided by Risk Management Solutions, Inc. (RMS) and Applied Insurance Research, Inc. (AIR), the two leading independent providers of such technology.[1] Most of the major insurers and reinsurers in the world use one or both of the RMS IRAS™ and the AIR CatMap™ models for quantifying potential losses, simulating expected losses over various periods, pricing risk transfer contracts, and structuring portfolios and capital allocations. The securitization process has favored the use of these models because of their widespread application in the insurance industry and because the vendors are independent of possible conflicts of interest in risk transfer transactions.

The leading models have been developed over at least ten years, reflecting data and knowledge from the scientific and engineering communities as well as underwriting and actuarial knowledge and actual

---

[1] Certain brokers and direct reinsurers have developed catastrophe modeling technology for their clients, including Guy Carpenter (EQECAT™), TPF&C (TopCat™), E.W. Blanch Co. (Catalyst™), Aon (Impact Forecasting™), Munich Re, and Swiss Re. RMS estimates that its current worldwide market share of insurer/reinsurer purchases of catastrophe risk modeling technology and advisory services is about 65%.

insurer experience. Basically, the systems compute expected losses from a specified financial perspective resulting from any or all potential catastrophic events from given perils for a specified set of exposures (such as the policies or locations covered in a securitization or reinsurance treaty). Figure 8-1 summarizes this process.

Figure 8-1 The Catastrophe Modeling Process

1. Define Portfolio Exposure	2. Loss/Risk Simulation	3. Catastrophe Model Output	4. Financial Modeling
• Locations	• Event definition	• Losses by historical and potential event	• Expected loss/risk profile for security
• Values	• Local hazard (windspeed)	• Average losses per period for portfolio or any layer	• Simulated yield profile for security
• Policy structures	• Vulnerability of exposures	• Uncertainty measures	• Uncertainty measures
• Reinsurance terms	• Financial loss to portfolio	• Losses by individual exposure unit	
	• Simulation of thousands of individual events ("stochastic set")		

Catastrophe models were originally developed to reflect the perspective of a primary insurer (policy level) or reinsurer (treaty or facultative). Recently, these perspectives have been extended to include the issuer of a catastrophe-linked security or an investor. The key analyses and outputs, however, are common for both traditional insurance/reinsurance and securitization applications. The RMS models compute the expected loss from each of several thousand individual events (earthquakes, hurricanes, or other covered perils), resulting in a cumulative distribution of expected mean losses (see figure 8-2). Using the calculated uncertainty (resulting from parameter uncertainty, process uncertainty, and correlated risk in the modeled portfolio), the model outputs a continuous "Occurrence Exceeding Probability" (OEP™) representing the probability of loss to the portfolio of any specified amount or greater in a specified period and an "Aggregate Exceeding Probability" (AEP™) representing the same perspective but reflecting the combination of multiple events (see figure 8-3).

Figure 8-2 Mean Loss Distribution

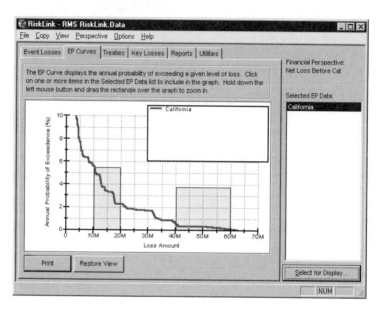

Figure 8-3 OEP™ and AEP™ Distributions

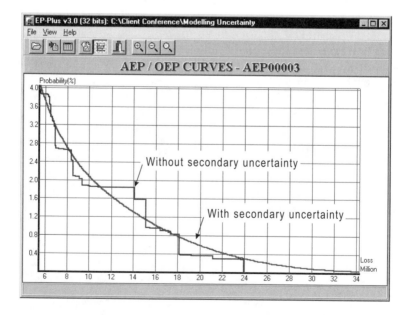

Figure 8-4 summarizes the specific output that is most valuable in securities transactions. Not surprisingly, the same output parameters are used by insurance and reinsurance underwriters in the traditional risk transfer markets.

Figure 8-4 Key Modeling Output

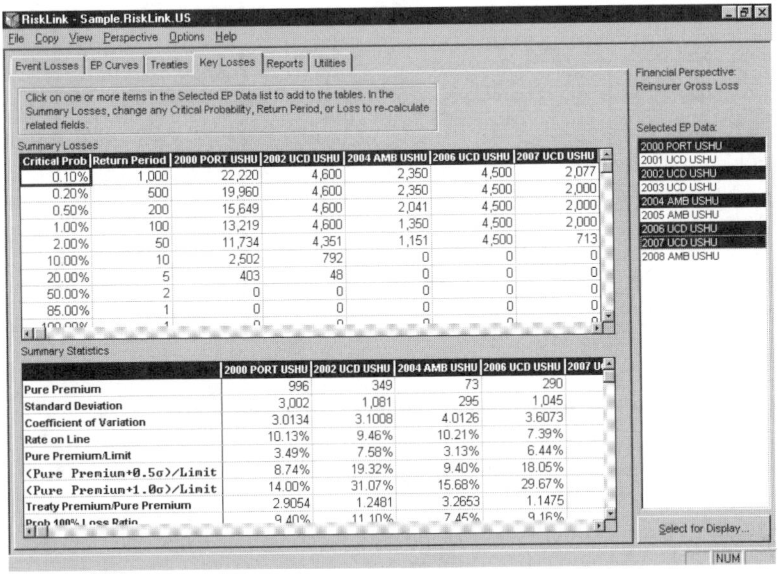

RiskLink - Sample.RiskLink.US

File Copy View Perspective Options Help

Event Losses | EP Curves | Treaties | Key Losses | Reports | Utilities

Click on one or more items in the Selected EP Data list to add to the tables. In the Summary Losses, change any Critical Probability, Return Period, or Loss to re-calculate related fields.

Financial Perspective:
Reinsurer Gross Loss

Selected EP Data:
2000 PORT USHU
2001 UCD USHU
2002 UCD USHU
2003 UCD USHU
2004 AMB USHU
2005 AMB USHU
2006 UCD USHU
2007 UCD USHU
2008 AMB USHU

Summary Losses

Critical Prob	Return Period	2000 PORT USHU	2002 UCD USHU	2004 AMB USHU	2006 UCD USHU	2007 UCD USHU
0.10%	1,000	22,220	4,600	2,350	4,500	2,077
0.20%	500	19,960	4,600	2,350	4,500	2,000
0.50%	200	15,649	4,600	2,041	4,500	2,000
1.00%	100	13,219	4,600	1,350	4,500	2,000
2.00%	50	11,734	4,351	1,151	4,500	713
10.00%	10	2,502	792	0	0	0
20.00%	5	403	48	0	0	0
50.00%	2	0	0	0	0	0
85.00%	1	0	0	0	0	0
100.00%		0	0	0		

Summary Statistics

	2000 PORT USHU	2002 UCD USHU	2004 AMB USHU	2006 UCD USHU	2007 U
Pure Premium	996	349	73	290	
Standard Deviation	3,002	1,081	295	1,045	
Coefficient of Variation	3.0134	3.1008	4.0126	3.6073	
Rate on Line	10.13%	9.46%	10.21%	7.39%	
Pure Premium/Limit	3.49%	7.58%	3.13%	6.44%	
(Pure Premium+0.5σ)/Limit	8.74%	19.32%	9.40%	18.05%	
(Pure Premium+1.0σ)/Limit	14.00%	31.07%	15.68%	29.67%	
Treaty Premium/Pure Premium	2.9054	1.2481	3.2653	1.1475	
Prob 100% Loss Ratio	9.40%	11.10%	7.45%	9.16%	

Select for Display...

NUM

In addition to these key outputs, the modeling analyst typically develops a financial modeling of the specific security structure of the issue, translating direct portfolio loss from the catastrophe model into the expected impact on the issuer or the investor in the security. Figure 8-5 exemplifies this security modeling.

Each of the major models developed independently from the others, and each has advantages and disadvantages for particular applications. Typically, RMS is asked to demonstrate the effectiveness of its models by comparing modeled losses for historical events to actual losses sustained by a portfolio of risks (see figure 8-6) or by comparing modeled losses over time to historical experience or market expectations reflected by market prices for risk transfer (see figure 8-7). While the correlation of modeled versus actual losses depends on a number of factors, including the accuracy of exposure information and the accuracy of reported actual losses, the models have demonstrated sufficient credibility to provide investors with the confidence to participate in the risk alongside reinsurers that have the advantage of far longer experience.

Figure 8-5 Security Modeling

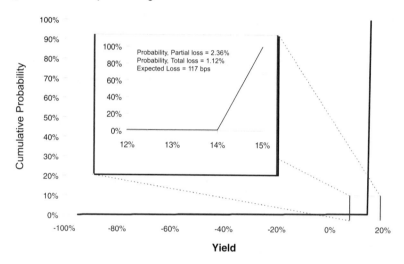

Figure 8-6 Comparison of RMS Modeled Losses versus Reported Losses for Individual Insurer Portfolios, Selected U.S. Hurricanes

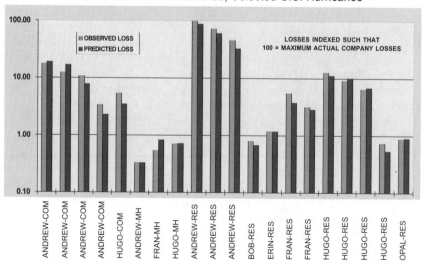

Figure 8-7 Comparison of RMS Modeled Losses versus U.S. Industry Reported
Losses, 1899-1996

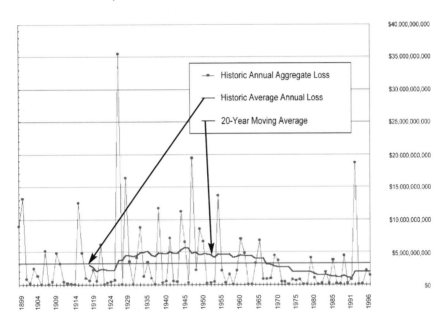

Commercial models that are currently available and widely used address insured property catastrophe risk for several regions and perils, as summarized in table 8-1. Presumably, similar models will be developed for other property and casualty risks as demand for traditional and securitization purposes grows. At RMS, we envision a spectrum of models as depicted in table 8-2.

Modeling has served a number of purposes in early securitization transactions, including providing a common risk communication mechanism for issuers and investors. A key concern of investors has been that they obtain the same level of risk quantification as the issuers have, as well as understanding how the traditional risk transfer markets (such as treaty reinsurance) measure, structure, and price such risk.

Table 8-1 Commercial Catastrophe Model Availability

Region	Earthquake	Hurricane	Other Wind	Other Perils
U.S.	X	X	X	X
Canada	X		X	X
Central America	Partial	Partial		
South America	Partial			
United Kingdom	X		X	X
Western Europe	X		X	X
Scandinavia			Partial	
Eastern Europe				
Caribbean	X	X		X
Pacific Islands	Partial	Partial		
Australia/NZ	X	(Typhoon)		X
Japan	X	(Typhoon)		X
China	X	(Typhoon)		X
Other Asia	Partial	Partial		

Table 8-2 Expected Model Availability

Market Sector	Application	Risks/Perils
Corporate risk	Enterprise (integrated) risk	Custom model of enterprise
	Insurance effectiveness	All insured
	Trading risk	
Insurance	All property catastrophe	Natural, man-made perils
	Property noncatastrophe	Fire, crime, etc.
	Volatile casualty risks	Product liability, etc.
	Reinsurance credit risk	All
	Enterprise (integrated) risk	Custom model of enterprise
Reinsurance	Enterprise (integrated) risk	Custom model of enterprise
	Treaty portfolio diversification	All
	Security cession/investment	All
Securities	Individual security simulation	All
	Risk correlation/new assets	All

Key factors driving the importance of modeling have included:

- low frequency of loss/lack of sufficient historical data for relevant statistical analysis of risk
- investor desire for a risk perspective from an independent source
- investor desire to compare and correlate risk from various securities
- lack of risk quantification modeling by traditional rating agencies
- widespread use of catastrophe modeling by traditional risk transfer markets
- market perception that modeling technology is increasingly effective in defining risk and potential losses

By using the same modeling technology, various participants in the risk transfer process can understand the perspectives of other constituents as well as communicate risk and return issues objectively. Figure 8-8 depicts the various parties in the process and their interaction using models or their output.

Figure 8-8 Interaction of Constituents through Modeling

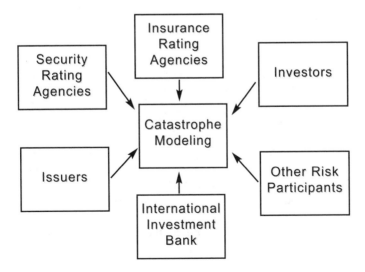

Analogies and Early Lessons

The asset class most commonly compared with insurance is the mortgage-backed securities (MBS) market. Like insurance-linked securities, MBS issues may represent many individual properties, with mortgages underwritten by one or more issuers. Similarly, the investor community demanded modeling of risk and securities yield, resulting in the MBS market from such factors as mortgage prepayment. Yet there the similarities seem to end. In the MBS market, risk diversification and risk management are accomplished through adherence to relatively simple rating agency models and guidelines for geographic and value distribution and certain credit enhancements. Prepayment risk models have been developed by intermediaries and investment banks, and these models are sufficiently similar that the choice of prepayment model does not typically affect an issue's marketability. Investors even have their own models. The complexity and various issues surrounding insurance risk, on the other hand, have favored the use of independent models provided by specialists.

Certain other securitized cash flows, such as credit card receivables, student loan repayments, and various asset-backed securities, rely on modeling for a common quantification of particular parameters. The investor community is therefore experienced at understanding the application of such models and in developing its own models for gaining additional and proprietary insights.

The question of which transaction represents the first true insurance risk securitization issue is debatable, but the first several transactions nevertheless had one common parameter: they were nonrated, private placement transactions. Early examples include transactions done by Citicorp for Hanover Re, "piggyback" contracts written by offshore investment funds as pro-rata participations alongside traditional reinsurers, and private placements made by groups such as Guy Carpenter, Centre Financial Products, and others on behalf of primary insurance issuers. These first transactions used little or no modeling, with the exception that the issuer typically provided its internal actuarial projections of expected loss probabilities based on its proprietary underwriting practices and in some cases using commercial modeling output. These transactions involved risks located in Asia, the United States, and Europe.

Subsequently, a number of transactions have been brought to market by investment banks and have been reviewed and rated by Duff & Phelps, Fitch, Moody's, and Standard & Poor's. These transactions, including Georgetown Re (St. Paul Re), Residential Re (USAA), Parametric Re (Tokio Marine/Swiss Re), and Trinity Re (Centre Solutions), have employed modeling extensively, both as the mechanism for risk quantification and as the key driver for the ratings. Transactions in process include portfolios of risk in multiple regions exposed to multiple perils (extending beyond the property catastrophe focus of earlier transactions). From a modeling perspective, several key lessons have come from these transactions:

- Rating agency due diligence of modeling methodology and application is extensive, reflecting the degree of presumed rating agency reputation exposure to and potential liability in the modeling quality.

- Investor due diligence of the modeling methodology and application is equally thorough. Investors place a great deal of emphasis on the modeling.

- Both rating agencies and investors have expressed a desire to standardize structures and modeling methods.

- The rating applied to a security reflects the agency's perception of the effectiveness of the model in defining risk for that particular region and peril as well as the modeled risk profile of the underlying exposures.

- Several major investors view their use of modeling as a mechanism that will help them to develop diversified portfolios of insurance-linked securities holdings, potentially driving market demand for such securitization.

The Current Formula for Success

Recent transactions that have used accepted commercial modeling such as RMS, that have been rated by a major rating agency, and that have been marketed by a leading investment bank have been oversubscribed. Although the full cost to the issuers of some early securities may have been higher than the traditional reinsurance market might have charged in its current soft state, the cost of the capital market alternative is coming down as the process becomes more standardized and as the investor community gains confidence in its understanding of the risks.

With respect to risk quantification, a prospective new issuer should build upon the established formula for success. This formula includes:

- Electronic exposure data that are at a market standard of resolution and defensible accuracy (such as is acceptable to leading reinsurers for similar transactions, typically either policy-specific or zip-code aggregation) and that are verified by an independent third party.

- Choice of a model that is already known to the rating agencies.

- Modeling analysis performed by a third party that is independent of the transaction.

- Modeling output that represents the format and content expected by investors, based on their recent experience with other securities issues.

- Disclosure of sufficient exposure information that investors can independently verify the risk quantification summarized in the prospectus.

Expected Developments in the Use of Models in Risk Securitization

Insurance industry expectations for the impact of securitization and capital markets investment run the gamut. The issue has been discussed for years, and the current debate will likely be over only when a major change occurs in the traditional markets as a result of securitization.

Change has already occurred. Securitization has changed modeling, modeling has changed securitization, and both are having a significant impact on traditional risk transfer markets. For example:

- The cost of a potential securitization is a new comparative benchmark for assessing reinsurance costs.

- Insurers and reinsurers analyzing their catastrophe risks for possible transfer are now typically preparing the data and modeling in anticipation of securitizations as potential alternatives.

- New generations of models are being developed to address specific issues raised by rating agencies and investors in the securitization process.

- New reinsurance companies are being formed to act specifically as conduits for securitization.

As the market matures and there becomes a large number of primary and secondary market securities for investors to choose from, the major investors will build and manage portfolios of these investments. They will want to measure and monitor the risk correlation or diversification between insurance-linked securities, and they will want to similarly track the correlation of risk between these securities and other assets in their portfolios. As a result, we foresee the following developments for modeling:

- The market will increasingly demand standardized exposure definition, and that demand will probably drive a continued consolidation toward the use of one or a few modeling approaches and technologies. Insurers and reinsurers will support these trends in order to ensure flexibility in their access to capital.

- Models will become increasingly sophisticated as the structure and type of securities and the growing expectations of the investor market drive innovation.

- Commercial models will be developed for many risks now quantified only through traditional underwriting and actuarial methods as the potential for securitization drives such development. These new models should include any risks for which the traditional markets appear to charge a volatility premium.

- Models must become capable of computing risk correlation across various risks and lines of business. These risks may all be included in individual securities issues, and they will certainly be present in investors' portfolios.

- What role the traditional rating agencies will play in the process must be resolved in the long term. Currently, some transactions are being marketed as nonrated. Since modeling has become so important, the rating agencies may consider development of their own modeling methods, or they may choose to work more closely with the independent modeling analysts. Alternatively, the investor market may demand the status quo, as it ensures that the modeling and analytics have been reviewed by a capable and unbiased source.

All indications from early market transactions point to a key role for modeling and to the importance of the independence of the modeling analysts from the transaction itself. Each of the leading providers of modeling and related services appears to be committed to the securitization market. It is therefore likely that as the market grows and clarifies its norms and expectations, modeling will retain a central role.

Insurance Risk Securitization, Model Robustness, and the Convergence of Event and Credit Risk: A Rating Analyst's View

David K. A. Mordecai
AIG Risk Finance—formerly of Fitch IBCA

Insurance- and reinsurance-linked securities have emerged as a new asset class for portfolio managers, as the cyclical dynamics of reinsurance pricing promise persistent periods of excess returns to the yield-hungry debt markets. Essentially, insurance-linked securities issued in the debt markets attempt to arbitrage the difference in pricing between comparable debt market–priced credit risk and "natural" event risk priced in the reinsurance market.

Event risk is priced in three markets: the insurance/reinsurance market, the debt markets, and the equity markets. Each market prices comparable expectations of risk differently. Much as institutional, regulatory, tax, and pricing conventions drive interest rate and equity price anomalies, capital contraints, regulatory frictions (risk-based capital treatment), and risk-adjusted pricing (economic value at risk) disparities motivate arbitrage between the insurance and capital markets.

Capital Market Approaches to Catastrophic Risk

Capital market approaches to catastrophic reinsurance risk include traditional reinsurance, contingent bank financing, and capital market securitizations such as insurance-linked credit swap financing, synthetic reinsurance, and third-party event risk swaps. Traditional reinsurance typically involves direct payment from a reinsurer to a ceding insurer if a defined event occurs. Contingent bank financing is a liquidity facility provided to an insurer in exchange for a facility fee and interest paid on the drawn amount. Credit risk securitization or insurance-linked credit swap financing involves investment-grade fixed-income securities held by a special purpose vehicle (SPV), where the securities may be called by the insurance company in exchange for surplus notes or debt issued by the insurance company. Synthetic reinsurance issuance is commonly referred to as a catastrophe-linked bond or simply a "catastrophe bond," that is, a reinsurance treaty–linked structured note issued by an SPV (see figure 9-1). Third-party event risk swaps are structured or "flow" trades between insurers and a counterparty involving an exchange of cashflows or securities triggered by a catastrophic event.

Figure 9-1 Catastrophe Bond Structure

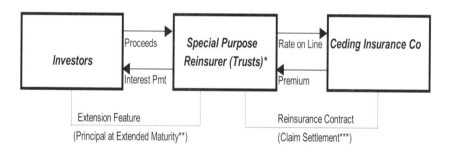

*May involve collateral and defeasance accounts with basis and/or total return swaps
**If principal protected with zero-coupon treasury strips (or treasury-forward obligations
***Triggered by attachment point as specified in reinsurance contract terms

Insurance derivatives are in many ways analogous to credit derivatives, in particular, default options and total return swaps. In fact, default options and credit swaps could be considered a form of insurance, similar to bond insurance. Options represent market event insurance, that is, a hedging and portfolio insurance vehicle identical in principle to stop-loss reinsurance. Forms of principal protection and defeasance, such as guaranties, treasuries, and forward obligations, represent credit insurance. These instruments all serve as substitutes or complements for credit and portfolio insurance supplied by the monoline or specialty financial insurance companies. Bottom line: insurance treaties as contingent claims are, in essence, derivative instruments, and conversely, derivatives are, in essence, insurance.

There are essentially two kinds of reinsurance treaties: facultative treaties and event-trigger treaties. A facultative treaty is a proportional reinsurance treaty in which the reinsurer shares equally in the premiums written and claims incurred by the primary insurer. In this sense, a facultative treaty is like a blanket policy for the primary or "ceding" insurer. Catastrophe bonds are typically structured around an event-trigger treaty. These reinsurance treaties are essentially swaps, and credit risk and default swaps employ a modeling approach similar to modeling catastrophe risk. The approach, adopted from extreme value theory, plays a particularly important role in the pricing of reinsurance contracts, especially those involving low-probability, high-severity events. For example, the Catastrophe Excess of Loss Cover per Event, or CatXL, reinsurance treaty corresponds in financial option theory to a bull spread, with the market loss ratio as the reference asset.

There has been discussion of linking cat bond structures to oil spills, industrial accidents, satellite risk, and a host of other insured risks. Yet the rated catastrophe-linked bonds now trading in the market all reference "acts of God" or natural disasters, specifically windstorm and seismic events. Also, at present, insurance regulators have restricted debt treatment for investments in cat bonds by insurance companies to natural disaster–related bonds rated by one of the four Nationally Recognized Securities Rating Organizations (NRSROs). Of the three rated cat bonds issued in 1997, one is hurricane-related; the other two are earthquake-related.

Cat bond structures fall into three broad categories: book-of-business, index-based, and parametric trigger structures. Cat bond investors can experience losses to either principal or interest, depending on the covenants of the bond. The book-of-business structure securitizes a portion of a ceding insurer's policies. The index-based structure attaches to an index of claims or losses as the reference asset. Losses to bondholders in both of these structures are triggered by the level of losses from an event above the referenced trigger or attachment point. A parametric trigger structure triggers losses to the bond based either on some inferred natural parameter, such as the magnitude and location of an earthquake, or by some other measure more directly related to the damage incurred in a region, such as measured ground motion from an earthquake occurrence. Of the two parametric triggers, the latter, although more complicated, presents fewer estimation problems and therefore provides more reliable model estimates and more predictable expected cashflows.

Actuarial and Stochastic Modeling in Catastrophe Analysis

Rating agencies and sophisticated cat risk investors assess expected bond performance first by analyzing the data used to create a model for estimating long-run odds of occurrence of a catastrophic event. Second, they evaluate the model structure and implementation in using the data to estimate the event risk. The model must adhere to standard practices. Third, they examine the structure of the bond. Not only must the structure be coherent, but the data must be accurate and complete. All three elements must be reasonable and consistent.

The growing interest in the capital markets for catastrophic risk securities is evident (see table 9-1). To complement or compete with the Property Claim Services (PCS) option contracts trading on the Chicago Board of Trade (CBOT), other exchanges have introduced rival indexes and futures. In 1996, the California Earthquake Authority (CEA) withdrew its $1.5 billion issue when Berkshire Hathaway bought the entire deal directly. Six months after the $68.5 million principal-protected Georgetown Re issue, heavy demand from investors more than doubled the at-risk portion of the USAA/Residential Re transaction. During that same period, the Swiss Re Earthquake Fund, an SPV, issued a bond with a trigger referencing losses as reported by PCS. A few months later, in a yield-hungry environment, another investment bank managed to place a bond triggered by a ten-year bet on the magnitude and location of an earthquake around Tokyo, the geographic region responsible for six to seven percent of the world's earthquakes. Then, in the spring of 1998, Aon Capital Markets successfully placed Pacific Re, a five-year Japanese typhoon bond with a moving attachment point. That was followed by the completion of a second USAA bond by Merrill Lynch and two other transactions by Goldman Sachs, one based on U.S., nationally distributed, multiple perils for a large reinsurer, the other involving the residual value of a leased fleet for Toyota. Various other issuers have announced plans for multi-year, multi-event, and index-based securitizations. Security structures with contingent features, such as the 300 million SF Winterthur interest-at-risk convertible issue, have generated interest as well.

Table 9-1 Completed Catastrophic Risk Securitizations

Issuer/Ceding Company	Amount	Instrument	SPV	Issue Date	Rated	Issuance
Credit Risk Securitizations						
Nationwide Mutual Insurance Co	$392 Mill	Contingent Surplus Notes	Nationwide CSN Trust	Feb-95		Mutual Funds, etc.
Arkwright Mutual Insurance Co	$100 Mill	Contingent Surplus Notes	Arkwright CSN Trust	May-96		Mutual Funds, etc.
Synthetic Reinsurance						
AIG	$10-25 Mill	Event-Linked Bond	Offshore Reinsurance Co	Apr-96		Single Investor
USAA (Book of Business)	$477 Mill	Event Loss-Based Attachment*	Residential Reinsurance Ltd	Jun-97	X	144A Private
Swiss Re (PCS Index-Based)	$140 Mill	Event Loss-Based Attachment*	Swiss Re Earthquake Fund	Jul-97	X	144A Private
Swiss Re (Parametric Trigger)	$100 Mill	Magnitude/Location Trigger*	Parametric Re	Nov-97	X	144A Private
Hannover Re	DM100 Mill	Life Acquisition Costs	LI	Apr-98		Private
Yasuda F&M	$80 Mill	Loss with Moving Attachment*	Munich	Apr-98	X	144A
USAA	$450 Mill	Event Loss-Based Attachment*	Residential Reinsurance Ltd	Jun-98	X	144A
F&G Re	$54 Mill	U.S.-Based Property/Casualty	Mosaic Re	Jul-98	X	144A
		* Multiple-tranche Principal-at-Risk				
OTC Swaps						
Mitsui F&M	$30 Mill	Tokyo Earthquake (Parametric Re Index)	Goldman/Swiss Re	Apr-98		Private
XLMidOcean Re		U.S.-Caribbean Earthquake/Wind	Goldman/Merrill/Swiss Re/ Lehman	Aug-98		Private
Other Structures						
Hannover Re	$100 Mill	Portfolio-Linked Swap		Nov-96		Institutional
St. Paul Companies	$68.5 Mill	Loss-Linked Notes	Georgetown Re	Dec-96		Institutional
RLI Corporation	$50 Mill	Catastrophe-Linked Equity Puts		Oct-96		Centre Re
Winterthur Insurance Company	$399 Mill	Convertible Sub with Interest-at-risk		Jan-97		Institutional/Retail
JUA (State Catastrophe Fund)	$200 Mill	Contingent Financing Structure	JUA	May-97		Bank Syndicates
FWUA (State Catastrophe Fund)	$400 Mill	Contingent Financing Structure	FWUA	Aug-97		Bank Syndicates
Lane Financial/Presidio (PXRE)		Equity	INVR I	Dec-95		
Sedgwick Lane Financial	$40 Mill	Original Discount Floating Rate Note	SLF I	Feb-97		

Noteworthy Transactions Announced

Issuer/Ceding Company	Amount	Instrument	SPV	Announce Date	Rated	Issuance
California Earthquake Authority	$1.5 Bill	Withdrawn Securitization	CEA	1996		Berkshire Hathaway

During the same 12- to 18-month period, the weather derivatives market has grown to surpass $3 billion of notional amount outstanding. Several transactions close each week, ranging in size from $500,000 to over $25 million. AIG Risk Finance, in particular, has been a pioneer with its STORM product, which embeds a basket of weather derivatives and other market risk derivatives into a hybrid insurance policy. Weather derivative-backed bonds have been proposed and are being attempted by entities such as the Investor's Guaranty Fund of Bermuda. Weather derivative-backed bonds or notes are securities issued by an offshore special purpose vehicle, usually domiciled in Bermuda or the Cayman or Jersey Islands for tax and insurance law purposes and generally capitalized with a master swap agreement and collateralized with U.S. treasuries or other investment-grade securities. The entity then enters into a series of derivative transactions—in this case, weather derivatives—with a counterparty or counterparties, and the bonds or notes are issued against the performance of these derivative transactions.

These products offer enhanced yields for investors and may provide both diversification opportunities and new capital for insurers. Yet the need to assess the risk of this emerging asset class has led to demand for stochastic models that can reliably and accurately represent the risk of loss from a catastrophic event. In fact, according to a recent *Wall Street Journal* article, insurance regulators are contemplating increasing their reliance on these models for setting rates. The question of the hour thus becomes, "How can we evaluate the performance of these models?"

This chapter addresses the essence of Fitch IBCA's approach to evaluating model performance from a due diligence and ratings perspective: *model robustness*. In the evaluation of stochastic or random event models, the robustness of a model can be described as the insensitivity or persistence of model outputs to changes in model inputs. This is the key feature of any statistical or probability estimation model that determines how well model estimates perform on average as a best guess or approximation of the future losses from a catastrophic event.

A robust model minimizes model risk. Conceptually and in practice, we can discuss model risk as having two components: process risk and parameter risk. Process risk is minimized when hypothesized assumptions reasonably represent the true nature of actual events (the underlying process). This dimension of model risk is a function both of the selection of distribution assumptions and the estimation of parameters for those distributions. Parameter risk is minimized as the number of simulated draws from a distribution is increased. In other words, if the hypothesized assumptions are reasonably accurate, then as the number of iterations becomes sufficiently large, the simulation estimates should converge to the long-run behavior of the actual physical phenomena being modeled. This defines model robustness, that is, how reliable model estimates are as long-run averages of event occurrences and magnitudes.

Sensitivity Analysis: The Key to Evaluating Model Robustness

Understanding the following concepts is essential to evaluating a model and presenting its results in the context of rating catastrophic risk securities. First, the analyst must translate a model simulation of a random event (which is based on correlations derived from inferences of historical observed events) into a rating assignment. In turn, the rating is associated with the risk of loss from the potential realization of an actual event. It is critical to draw a sharp distinction between probability ("odds" or "likelihood") of an actual event versus the observed frequencies from the model simulation.

In addition to inspecting the underlying data for accuracy, consistency, and completeness, Fitch IBCA evaluates the underlying technical integrity of the model from the perspective of process risk minimization. Fitch IBCA assesses a random event model on the basis of (a) model structure (i.e., model design and procedural implementation) and (b) model specification (i.e., selection of distribution assumptions and parameter estimation).

In evaluating model structure, Fitch IBCA reviews the mathematical functions used to approximate the interactions between simulated storm values. Fitch IBCA compares them to current academic and industry practices to judge if they reasonably and adequately represent event characteristics. Some of these interactions are modeled as probability distributions, while others are functions measured or derived from current research. Evaluating model specification includes an assessment of the appropriateness of (a) the probability distribution assumptions selected and (b) the estimation methods employed to fit the parameters of those distributions.

To arrive at a level of comfort regarding process risk, Fitch IBCA evaluates the robustness of model estimates in the following manner: (a) worst-case "what-if" scenarios (outlier analysis); (b) back-testing/out-of-sample tests; and (c) sensitivity analysis using alternative distributions. Random event models and their resulting loss distribution estimates tend to be sensitive to tail specification, that is, to extreme value estimation.

Tail specification is a critical factor for the reliability or robustness of the model estimates as long-run averages of loss occurrence.

Fitch IBCA applies a simulation sensitivity analysis to simulations that employ alternate distribution assumptions for both frequency-of-event occurrence and magnitude-of-event occurrences. Based on the above tests and other considerations, the Fitch IBCA analyst may analytically modify the location of the attachment point or the shape of the exceedence curve (see sidebar). The modification of the exceedence curve to reflect bias in the model estimates of loss (or risk of loss), depending on the assessment of the model's robustness or lack thereof. In other words, adjustments are based on the relative sensitivity of the model to modified assumptions.

Credit analysis and derivative pricing are both exercises in variance estimation. Quantifying uncertainty is always challenging, often problematic, and sometimes unfeasible. As a general rule, rigorous robustness testing requires an estimate to be modeled as a probability distribution with a smooth, disperse surface and finite variance. Models that generate point or spiked estimates tend to grossly understate uncertainty. In other words, these models are "infinitely" sensitive to tail observations or "outliers." In addition, the distribution modeled must match the actual event process. These conditions dictate the kinds of parameters that can be used as triggers. Parameter triggers that employ loss-related damage functions are generally superior to parameter triggers that attempt to model predictive estimates of event locations and magnitudes.

Predictive estimates tend to have very large, nonlinear confidence bands (very large variance) and usually require a larger sample of reliable data than is feasibly available. In addition, the estimation and identification problems for some parameter triggers limit the effectiveness of most model calibration methods. Ironically, model diagnostics tend to be even more important for predictive parameter triggers, especially given common problems with autocorrelation and heteroskedasticity. Confounding effects from measurement error in the data employed to specify estimates in the model tend to result in estimation error and model misspecification that, under the circumstances, can be extremely difficult, if not impossible, to rectify.

Damage-based parameter triggers tend to resolve many complications inherent to modeled event occurrence estimates. Often, natural physical relations approximated by damage functions limit the effects of uncertainty around the model estimate of occurrence. In addition, loss and damage data, which tend to be more readily available and testable, can be used to independently calibrate the model and hence reduce model

Employing the Exceedence Curve in the Fitch IBCA Analysis

Fitch IBCA focuses its analysis around the attachment point, which is set by the transaction structure. Fitch IBCA uses the points provided by the modeling firm to construct an approximated exceedence curve using linear interpolation. The points on the exceedence curve near the attachment point are employed to compute expected losses as a weighted average.

1. Losses from events of a specified magnitude are weighted by the likelihood of occurrence for the event of that magnitude => *"expected losses"*:

   {odds of event at loss level}*{incremental loss incurred by that event}

2. These weighted values (*expected losses*) are then summed.

3. The sum of the weighted values is divided by the *"total number of loss events"* (simulated event scenarios contributing to losses) => *"expected loss severity"* (expressed as both a dollar value and as a percentage of principal-at-risk):

   {expected losses}/{total number of loss events}

4. The *"cumulative probability of loss"* (the sum of event increments contributing to each specified loss level) is multiplied by the expected loss severity (as a percentage of principal-at-risk) => *"cumulative expected loss"*:

   {cumulative probability of loss}*{expected loss severity}

5. The *cumulative expected loss* (i.e., summed probable losses to principal) value is compared to corporate bond defaults and recoveries to assign a rating.

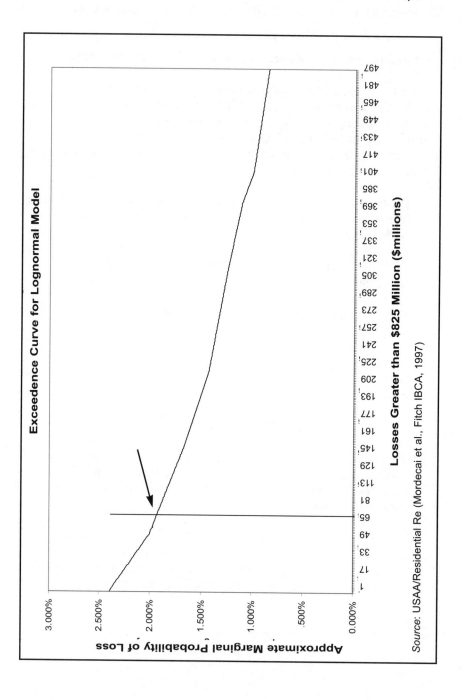

Exceedence Curve for Lognormal Model

Losses Greater than $825 Million ($millions)

Approximate Marginal Probability of Loss

Source: USAA/Residential Re (Mordecai et al., Fitch IBCA, 1997)

risk. Since damage parameters are conditioned upon the occurrence of an event, damage-based models employ a distribution of all feasible events for a region, resulting in a smoother, more robust distribution. Finally, knowledge about the structural relationships related to damage parameters tends to be more reliable and complete than knowledge about the physical processes related to occurrence parameters.

Other risks inherent to insurance-linked bonds include basis risk, moral hazard, and adverse selection. As with many derivative instruments, insurance-linked securities can exhibit tracking error, or "basis risk." Depending on the structure, basis risk can either be retained by the issuer (ceding insurer) or passed on to the investors. Issuers tend to prefer book-of-business triggers, because they minimize basis risk for the issuer relative to changes in the risk profile of future policies or to the aggregate risk profile of an index. Investors tend to prefer index-based triggers, unless the issuer has the ability to change the profile of the index. Issuers often like the level of confidentiality afforded to them by index-based triggers, but are averse to exposing their portfolio of policies to basis risk from an index trigger. Parametric triggers share some of the same issues as index-based triggers.

In the absence of adequate risk-retention language in the reps and warranties regarding the ceding insurer, all of these bond types are subject to varying degrees of risk shifting, such as moral hazard or adverse selection. Notably, this risk-retention mechanism is explicitly absent from structures with predictive parameter triggers. Also, predictive parameter triggers may exhibit the highest basis risk to either issuers or investors, depending on several factors, including the composition of the insurance portfolio, the policy types written by the ceding insurer, the precise trigger mechanism, and the degree of model estimation error. Even when loss data are limited, a damage-related trigger, correlated to loss retention–like covenants in a bond, may mitigate the incentives to improperly shift risk to bondholders.

The rigorous application of these principles to the analysis of random event modeling is central to an accurate and reliable assessment of catastrophic risk transactions. If this emerging asset class is to grow and mature, model robustness is a timely and important issue to consider, not only for rating agencies, but also for regulators, bankers, issuers, and investors.

Parallels Between Credit and Insurance Derivatives

For the same capacity and capital availability reasons existing in the property and casualty markets, institutional investors with excess "off-the-run" credit analysis capacity will conceivably enter the credit-enhanced note market (see figure 9-2) to compete with and potentially displace the traditional monoline portfolio insurers like Capmac, Ambac/MBIA, and FGIC. As the credit swaps market becomes broader, deeper, and more liquid, credit enhancement may become even more commonplace in the synthetics marketplace, especially for below-investment-grade issuers and counterparties. Rating agencies must strive to consistently assign ratings to comparable levels of credit risk for events in different markets. For that to happen effectively, rating analysts at the agencies must analytically compare the implied volatility of the default options embedded in these new debt instruments.

Figure 9-2 Credit-Linked Note Structure

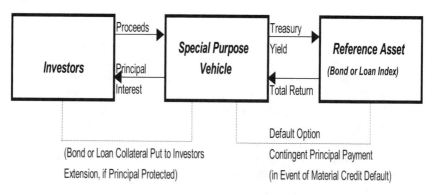

Credit derivatives in one form or another have enjoyed a long history in off-balance-sheet and nonrecourse structured financing as traditional contingent products. For example:

- Back-to-back loans have facilitated cross-border corporate borrowing.

- Backup lines of credit have contributed to the securitization of corporate credit by supporting commercial paper issuance.

- Other contingent credit issuances have served to guarantee project, equipment, and trade financing:
  - standby LOCs
  - forward contracts
  - limited guarantees
  - defeasance, escrow, reserve, and collateral accounts
  - backup and liquidity facilities

In their simplest form, credit derivatives involve an exchange of cashflows between two counterparties based on some underlying notional amount, typically related to a traditional credit facility. Just like other derivative products, simple credit derivatives can be broadly classified as swaps, options, or forwards. More complex structures combine simpler credit derivatives to incorporate the correlation of state-dependent payoffs.

Credit derivatives have traditionally existed, for at least twenty years, in the form of bond insurance and in other forms of credit protection constructed from more conventional credit facilities, such as special-purpose or standby letters of credit. More current credit derivative instruments, however, are specifically designed to strip out and trade credit risk, to have a well-defined payoff, and hence to be priced efficiently, based on the perceived risk of a specific credit event, such as a default. Increasingly, these over-the-counter, market-traded credit derivatives are replacing traditional credit facilities in special-purpose credit-enhanced structures.

For credit-enhanced synthetic or structured notes, an appropriately structured credit derivative can sometimes serve as a cost-effective substitute for or complement to a third-party financial guarantee, that is, credit or portfolio insurance. In this role, the credit derivative exchanges counterparty credit risk for the credit risk of the underlying asset. As the market for active counterparties becomes broader and deeper with entry, it will augment the greater liquidity and rational pricing of the current market for credit insurance.

Similar development can be observed in the parallel histories of insurance risk management and commodity price risk management, and its extension into financial market risk management, over the past 25 years. Alternative risk financing techniques, such as self-insurance, self-funding, financial reinsurance, and "captives," now common to the insurance industry, bear close resemblance to the structures emerging in the synthetics and credit derivatives markets.

Much as synthetic securities maximize collateral efficiency for purposes of investment and market risk allocation, market-based credit derivatives can potentially maximize collateral efficiency for credit enhancement purposes relative to traditional forms. For example, a total return swap provides off-market economic exposure to the credit risk of the underlying asset for a synthetic financing cost significantly lower than the market rate, especially for a lower-rated buyer of the swap. Insurance derivatives similarly serve as economic alternatives for regulatory and economic risk-based capital relief. From a contingent claims perspective, a reinsurance contract even shares many of the same analytic features as a credit swap or a default option. As extremal events, both credit default risk and catastrophic insurance risk are subsets of intermediated event risk. In fact, all risky debt claims, and insurance contracts as contingent claims, can be modeled as "knockout" or "barrier" options, though excess-of-loss reinsurance contracts and single-event catastrophe bonds tend to exhibit default behavior that is more discrete or "digital" in nature than a corporate credit instrument.

In short, interest rate and credit derivatives permit arbitrage of all of the following risk-adjusted credit premium relationships:

- default risk and credit sensitivity
- preferences for fixed-rate vs. floating-rate coupons
- term structure risk (volatility, i.e., duration and convexity)
- term structure of credit risk (i.e., the correlation and integration of credit risk and market risk)

More complete contracting via insurance, credit, equity, and other derivatives supplies investment opportunities to the marketplace that more efficiently capture the payoff distribution of an event, a specific pool of assets, particular industry structures, or the unique investment opportunity set of an individual firm. Creating fundamental option and portfolio theory applications for credit derivative products is leading to further development of the contingent claims analysis of firm value and default risk. These approaches, in turn, are leading to innovations in permanent financing for conventional and special-purpose insurance portfolios. Some of these contingent financing products (such as putable preferred) are based on derivative features that segregate or combine insurance event risk and credit risk elements. Products in development include basket options, credit spread options, and correlation products.

For example, a credit exchange bond allows an investor to earn excess returns relative to a traditional bond with comparable default risk. With this structure (see figure 9-3), the investor may achieve an enhanced return by assuming additional interest rate or call risk. A credit exchange bond is a basket trade, that is, an obligation issued by a financial intermediary in which the reference asset is the credit performance of a basket of underlying corporate bonds. In addition to an incremental spread paid during the option period, and a lower additional spread paid to the maturity of the bond, the investor will receive the cheapest of the underlying corporate bonds at option maturity.

Figure 9-3 Credit Exchange Bond Structure

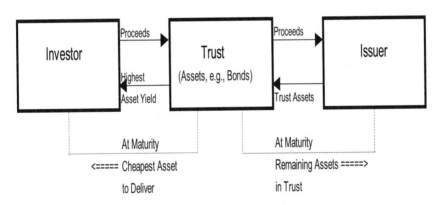

Simple credit option strategies include selling a covered call, selling a naked put, and hedging with credit puts. Selling a covered call is a yield enhancement strategy, where the risk is the opportunity cost if the credit spread tightens more than the amount of the yield enhancement, that is, the premium received from the sale of the call (see figure 9-4).

Selling a naked put enhances yield and lowers the average cost of the portfolio by selling an obligation to purchase bonds at a predetermined spread to treasuries (see figure 9-5). Here the risk is that the credit spread widens such that the loss from the exercised purchase obligation exceeds the yield enhancement (and funding cost savings).

Figure 9-4 Covered Call

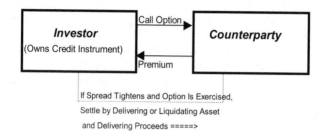

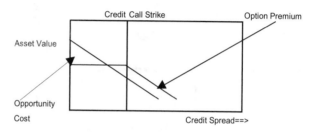

Figure 9-5 Naked Put

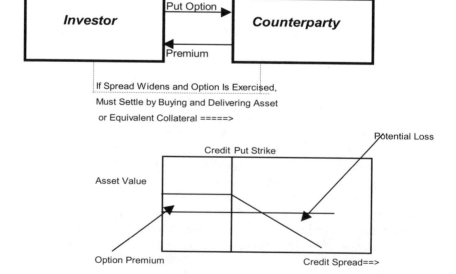

Hedging with credit puts provides credit protection by purchasing options payable in future periods. These features are common in many, if not most, repackaged or synthetic notes, especially those where the originator of the structure also serves as the counterparty that guarantees the minimum return to the trust that issues the notes (see figure 9-6). Whether these embedded features are priced as efficiently (i.e., competitively) as an implicit credit option by either the investor or the originator of the structure is an empirical question.

What's motivating these trades? The ability to build complex structures from simpler derivatives by balancing cost, credit, and pricing considerations:

- the role of "implicit leverage" and "all-in-cost" concepts in pricing and structuring
- credit or event spread intermediation (i.e., the certainty equivalent or "breakeven" spread)
- default substitution
- capital structure arbitrage

The breakeven spread on a risky debt instrument is the calculated yield spread to treasuries at which an investor is indifferent between investing in an instrument with a given level of credit or event risk versus investing in a risk-free instrument. Market spreads tend to exceed breakeven spreads for reasons related to regulation, risk aversion, liquidity, and taxes.

As with other derivative instruments, constructing and valuing these structures involves the use of default or event estimation applications like the Stein estimator and volatility estimation and simulation methodologies, like Markov Chain Monte Carlo algorithms and stratified sampling techniques. As a rating agency, Fitch IBCA, in addition to its ongoing due diligence of catastrophe risk modeling firms, has conducted research incorporating elements of JP Morgan's Creditmetrics and CSFP's Creditrisk+ models into its rating analytics. Creditmetrics employs a value-at-risk approach to default and recovery estimation. In contrast, Creditrisk+ employs an actuarial approach similar to the methodology used for insurance portfolios. More recently, McKinsey & Co. unveiled its Creditview product.

Figure 9-6 Synthetic Note Structures

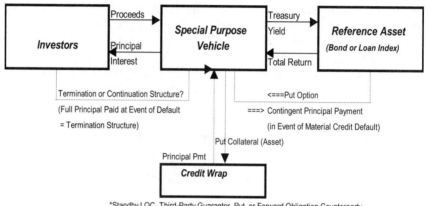

Swap-Dependent Structure (Wrapped)

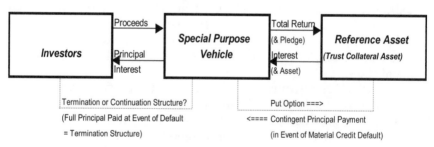

Swap-Dependent Structure

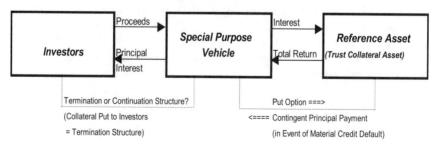

Swap-Independent Structure

Asset managers are increasingly focused on the spread between their weighted average cost of capital (WACC)—that is, the weighted average coupon (WAC) of their fixed obligations—and the weighted average price (WAP) and weighted average maturity (WAM) of assets in their portfolio. This has further stimulated the other side of yield management: the modeling and managing of expected losses using credit derivatives. Bankers and portfolio managers are adopting more sophisticated credit modeling approaches based on VaR or actuarial approaches. Similar market pressures are driving credit and bond underwriters to adopt financial and derivative market vehicles to expand capacity and lower cost. Insurance companies, in managing their investment portfolios and developing tailored investment products for the marketplace, are incorporating credit risk management along with asset-liability management technology. In other words, financial managers are thinking more like risk managers in their search for risk-adjusted return, and insurance companies are competing both in the capital markets and increasingly in the reinsurance market with new entrants.

Rating agencies and regulators mandate rigorous underwriting standards and capital requirements for financial guarantee insurers, based on perceived levels of underwriting risk. The result is that credit insurance tends to be a very capital-intensive sector of the insurance industry. Credit events are by their very nature extremal events (rare probabilistic events). Although analysts continue to use liability models, based on capital resources relative to underwriting exposures, more and more analysts are beginning to adopt models with an emphasis on assets in a credit insurer's portfolio, including the value of the assets that comprise unearned premiums. In the ongoing evolution of the credit, insurance, and asset swap markets, even rating agencies are being required to price assets and estimate event likelihood in order to derive credit risk and the probabilities of default. Expect this trend toward arbitrage between credit risk and event risk to persist as the market risk approach and the statistical risk approaches of the financial and insurance markets converge.

Index